# Manna-Feast, Vol. 2

## DAILY CONTEMPLATIONS FOR HUNGRY SOULS

REV. DR. OTIS MANNING

Library of Congress Control Number:
2025941854

ISBN#s
-PAPERBACK:
978-1-960594-35-8

-HARDBACK:
978-1-960594-68-6

-EBOOK:
978-1-960594-37-2

Publisher:
Rev. Dr. Otis Manning

# INTRODUCTION

I hope you have read Manna-Feast, Volume 1, which covers the first six months of the year, and made the Contemplations a part of your daily devotion time. If so, you should have expanded your knowledge of the Bible, gained some spiritual ammunition to defend yourself against the devil's attack, and have a more meaningful prayer life as you enjoy a closer relationship with God. There is no turning back; you are on your way to being conformed to the image of Christ.

Volume 2 continues this spiritual growth with rich content to dig deeper into the Word. In Hosea 4: 6, we are told, "My people are destroyed for lack of knowledge." This is how serious it is not to spend time in the Word of God, learning how to please Him, and benefit from all His promises. Knowledge of God is how we fulfill our purpose, be an overcomer, have an abundant life, and be a sharp instrument in God's hands. I am happy to be your teacher in helping you "rightly divide the word of truth." Of course, the Holy Spirit, the God of all wisdom, will be your ultimate guide and teacher.

As always, all scripture references are from the King James Version. Select a time and place, get alone with God, and be blessed.

# Day 182

*"A new season calls for new trees."*

*"Remember ye not the former things, neither consider the things of old"*(Isaiah 43:18).

A new season indicates a new atmosphere. This new season calls for you to be appreciative and sensitive to this newness. It means that the previous mentality and behaviors you had in the previous season may not necessarily accelerate you in the new one.

The same principle of not carrying old behaviors into a new season applies to the people you have around you. This doesn't mean they are bad people and you are cutting them off. That is not what you should do. However, when you see that certain people are drifting further from you, do not be alarmed, as it may indicate that their season in your life is over. You may try to hold on to them closely, but you cannot constantly carry the same people throughout your seasons. Not everyone can see you up close at your next level.

God is preparing new spaces for new trees to be planted. These can be people who will be your destiny helpers for the next steps ahead or people you will help push into their destiny. New seasons call for preparation; do not let your new seasons catch you unprepared. Ask God for wisdom to know how to navigate into the newness.

**For Contemplation**

1. Reflect on the first six months of the year. Can you identify persons God has removed from your life for your benefit?

**NOTES:**

___

___

___

**Prayer changes things and people; make it a priority.**

# Day 183

***"A distraction can turn into a main attraction."***

*"Let thine eyes look right on, and let thine eyelids look straight before thee. Ponder the path of thy feet, and let all thy ways be established. Turn not to the right hand nor to the left: remove thy foot from evil"* (Proverbs 4:25-27).

The spirit of distraction is now more rampant on the earth than ever before. Distractions can be easily seen or heard, which triggers our emotions to react to them. After that, the distractions form a part of our memory. Even though these distractions are present and we cannot avoid them, we must be aware of the aftereffects they can cause us.

We should never allow the distractions of the world to become our focus. The focus is to be ready for the coming of Jesus Christ. We should be focused on getting our hearts pure. The distractions are things that are external to God, so these external forces of darkness should not be able to dispel the light of God within us. The light of God within us should be the force that dispels all darkness. Let the light of God shine so that it becomes your main attraction. Keep your eyes on Jesus.

**For Contemplation**

1. Can you identify any instance in the last 6 months where a distraction came? How did you handle the situation?
2. Spend five minutes praying against the spirit of distraction.

**NOTES:**

______________________________

______________________________

______________________________

**Prayer changes things and people; make it a priority.**

# Day 184

***"Wayside things are not intended for you, but they can have an adverse effect on you."***

*"For I reckon that the sufferings of this present time are not worthy to be compared with the glory which shall be revealed in us"* (Romans 8:18).

There are things that may happen to us that do not come from God. This could be the presence of sin, or an open door to the enemy is present in our lives. These things can affect us, however, what the enemy meant for evil, God will turn it around for our good.

The Bible tells us that we should not be surprised when challenges and tribulations come our way. With these challenges we should be confident knowing that God will carry us through.

**For Contemplation**

1. Analyse your life and the patterns in your life. Can you identify any open doors? If yes, repent sincerely, shut them, and ask God to reveal if there is more you are not seeing.

**NOTES:**

**Prayer changes things and people; make it a priority.**

# Day 185

***"The fear of the Lord will drive you away from error."***

*"And Moses said unto the people, Fear not: for God is come to prove you, and that His fear may be before your faces, that ye sin not* (Exodus 20:20).

The fear of the Lord keeps us from sinning against Him. The fear of the Lord comes out of our adoration and love for Him. Just like loving someone and trying not to deliberately hurt them or do things that displease them. Instead, you try to always show them that you love them.

God is our Heavenly Father and He deserves our true love and devotion. Once you love Him, it is hard for you to blatantly commit sin. And if you do, the guilt you face will lead you to true repentance.

The fear of the Lord is the beginning of wisdom (Proverbs 9:10). This means that because you have the fear of the Lord, you have the wisdom to live a life that is according to the nature of God. This keeps you from living a life that pleases your flesh and instead pleases God. The fear of the Lord should be in all of us. As you fear Him, He will continue to trust you with His presence.

**For Contemplation**

1. Find five scriptures that speak about the fear of the Lord.

**NOTES:**

____________________________________________

____________________________________________

____________________________________________

**Prayer changes things and people; make it a priority.**

# Day 186

***"When you have problems, you will put down pride."***

*"The righteous cry, and the Lord heareth, and delivereth them out of all their troubles. The Lord is nigh unto them that are of a broken heart; and saveth such as be of a contrite spirit. Many are the afflictions of the righteous: but the Lord delivereth him out of them all"* (Psalm 34:17-19).

As you cry unto God in your time of trouble, it doesn't matter how you look or sound. When you are desperate and want to get out of a situation because you are tired of it, you will cry out. Pride in that moment dwindles, because it only wants you to behave as if you are better than and you have it all together. But as you are in need of help, and with God as your only Deliverer you have to ensure that even when your heart is broken, it can still reach out to Him.

*"The sacrifices of God are a broken spirit: a broken and a contrite heart, O God, thou wilt not despise"* (Psalm 51:17). The Lord will not turn you away in your state of brokenness. A broken spirit is a sacrifice unto Him, which means He takes delight in a broken spirit and He will receive you as you are. He will not reject you, even in your low states. When you need help, positions do not matter. When you need help, you need help.

**For Contemplation**

1. What is your posture when you are in need of something from God?
2. Is pride stopping you from crying out to God?

**NOTES:**

__________________________________________________

__________________________________________________

__________________________________________________

**Prayer changes things and people; make it a priority.**

# Day 187

***"Many persons call on the name of Jesus, but they do not know how to unlock the power within the name of Jesus."***

*"Wherefore, God also hath highly exalted Him, and given Him a name which is above every name: That at the name of Jesus every knee should bow, of things in heaven, and things in earth, and things under the earth; And that every tongue should confess that Jesus Christ is Lord, to the glory of God the Father"* (Philippians 2:9-11).

The name of Jesus is high above every other name and everything that has a name. His name applies to things bound to the earth, under it, and in the heavens. This is why we should pray in the name of Jesus: because power is held within His name. We can bind things on earth, under the earth, and forces that work against us that are situated in the heavens.

Many people call upon the name of Jesus, but their lack of understanding about the power of His name can cause them to use it ineffectively. It doesn't matter what comes up against you, the name of Jesus can reach and counteract it. When you speak the name of Jesus, remember that it is a name that has power to change any situation.

**For Contemplation**

1. As you read John 14:13-14 remember when you pray to seal your prayers "In Jesus Name".

**NOTES:**

______________________________________________

______________________________________________

______________________________________________

**Prayer changes things and people; make it a priority.**

# Day 188

***"If you are not bearing the fruit of the Spirit, you are not glorifying God."***

*"Ye shall know them by their fruits. Do men gather grapes of thorns, or figs of thistles? Even so, every good tree bringeth forth good fruit; but a corrupt tree bringeth forth evil fruit"* (Matthew 7:16-17).

The production of the fruit of the Spirit indicates that you are connected to God. It is not the signs or miracles that follow you. Remember that the gifts and calling of God are without repentance (Romans 11:29). This means that once God gives you a gift, they are irrevocable. He will not take them away from you. This is why you cannot use these signs to determine who is a good Christian.

The Bible tells us to examine the fruit they produce. If they are good, they will produce good fruit; if they are corrupt, then corrupt fruit will be seen. The fruits prove that God is getting the glory from your life because if you live a life set out by Him and allow Him to lead you, this will produce godly fruit.

**For Contemplation**

1. How do you determine whether someone is a good person or a bad person? Are you judging by their fruits?

**NOTES:**

________________________________________

________________________________________

________________________________________

**Prayer changes things and people; make it a priority.**

# Day 189

***"God loves a true worshipper."***

*"But the hour cometh, and now is, when the true worshippers shall worship the Father in spirit and in truth: for the Father seeketh such to worship Him. God is a Spirit: and they that worship Him must worship Him in spirit and in truth"* (John 4:23-24 ).

God loves those who desire to worship Him. The scripture says He seeks those who truly worship Him. As you worship Him, He will pour out His presence in different ways. His Spirit is infinite and indescribable, and it is impossible to be satisfied with His presence.

Worship is a response to God's revelation to us. How God reveals Himself to us fuels our worship. Our worship should not be driven by how much we can get from Him. We should first seek Him with our whole hearts, after which all other things will be added to us. There are different types of worship:

- YADAH: to worship with the extended hand. The giving of oneself in worship and adoration. To lift your hands unto the Lord. It carries the meaning of absolute surrender as a young child does to a parent stretching their hands and saying, "Pick me up; I'm all yours."
- TEHILLAH: to sing. This is the spontaneous singing of a new song. We can make melodies to the Lord, by singing what we hear in the Spirit or singing His word back to Him.
- BARAK: to kneel or to bow. This gives reverence to God as an act of showing that His presence is so glorious and we are His creations, giving honor to our Creator.
- HALAL: means to boast or celebrate in the Lord. Telling of all He has miraculously done.
- TOWDAH: giving thanks and adoration to God for what He has done and will do. An act of giving Him thanks.

- ZAMAR: to sing with instruments. Music plays a vital role in the presence of God. Music invokes a different atmosphere by the frequencies that are played.
- SHABACH: to shout unto the Lord with a voice of triumph. This is a loud adoration unto God.

Worshipping God is vital to our relationship with Him. We must always worship Him, no matter how we feel or what happens around us. A true worshipper of Yahweh worships despite external forces.

**For Contemplation**

1. We must first worship God in spirit and in truth, not just in the house of the Lord but in our lifestyle and how we treat others. What external factors affect how you worship God?
2. Does your worship differ on a good versus a bad day?

**NOTES:**

________________________________________

________________________________________

________________________________________

**Prayer changes things and people; make it a priority.**

# Day 190

***"You need to know how to cultivate the voice of God."***

*"For God speaketh once, yea twice, yet man perceiveth it not. In a dream, in a vision of the night, when deep sleep falleth upon men, in slumberings upon the bed; Then he openeth the ears of men, and sealeth their instruction"*( Job 33:14-16).

There is a possibility that we may not hear God's voice when He speaks. However, God will speak to us through different means. People often say, "My mind told me to do this." Sometimes, we attribute the voice of God to our own thoughts and simply bypass what we hear because we think it came from us. However, it could be God trying to tell us something.

We have to be sensitive to know when God is speaking to us. We have to learn to sense by the situations around us that He may be speaking to us. We have to learn to train our spirits to identify the voice and move of God. Fasting is a method that helps to clear our spirits, by causing our flesh to decrease so that we can hear His voice clearer. His voice is loud in His words. These help us to know that His Spirit is speaking to us because it will align with the words that are in the Bible. We cultivate the voice of God by spending time in His presence and being still in His presence.

**For Contemplation**

1. Are you able to identify the voice of God? What are the ways in which God speaks to you?

**NOTES:**

____________________________________________

____________________________________________

____________________________________________

**Prayer changes things and people; make it a priority.**

# Day 191

***"Sometimes you have to turn yourself from your own heart."***

*"The heart is deceitful above all things and desperately wicked: who can know it"* (Jeremiah 17:9)?

Our hearts are deceitful; hence, we cannot trust them. We cannot live our lives by following our hearts. If we give our hearts full control, they can lead us away from the heart of God.

Do not follow the desires of the heart to avoid ending up in detrimental circumstances. The heart carries the issues of life, so it is where the negative emotions that arise from our experiences on earth are stored. If we allow these negative emotions—hatred, anxiety, confusion, lust, jealousy, and pride—to take over and lead, then we are not living by the Spirit of God.

Once these emotions arise, the spirit of God within us will help us eradicate them and know how to respond to the situation correctly. Do not trust your own heart; trust the heart of God.

**For Contemplation**

1. As you meditate on Proverbs 3:5 in every situation you encounter, remember to use your heart to trust in God.

**NOTES:**

______________________________________________

______________________________________________

______________________________________________

**Prayer changes things and people; make it a priority.**

# Day 192

***"When you begin to live for God, you will be the one who will set the standard in your family."***

*"Seeing that Abraham shall surely become a great and mighty nation, and all the nations of the earth shall be blessed in him? For I know him, that he will command his children and his household after him, and they shall keep the way of the Lord, to do justice and judgement; that the Lord*

*may bring upon Abraham that which he hath spoken of him"* (Genesis 18:18-19).

God knew Abraham, and so because God knew the heart of Abraham; he was chosen by God to be the 'father of the faith'. Abraham is the first Patriarch of Judaism. He was the first person God made an official covenant with for the people of Israel.

So, God chose Abraham because He was sure that Abraham would tell his children and future generations the ways of the Lord. God was sure that Abraham would carry on His principles here on earth.

Abraham became God's standard to an entire nation, even up to this present day. The characteristics of Abraham are admirable and highlighted.

**For Contemplation**

1. Can God trust you to influence those around you to keep His way and command your generation to serve Him?
2. What are some characteristics you have that can benefit God?

**NOTES:**

______________________________________________

______________________________________________

______________________________________________

**Prayer changes things and people; make it a priority.**

# Day 193

***"The earth does not have the power to bring forth bud, it needs the rain from heaven."***

*"And also I have withholden the rain from you, when there were yet three months to the harvest: and I caused it to rain upon one city, and caused it not to rain upon another city: one piece was rained upon, and the piece whereupon it rained not withered"* (Amos 4:7 ).

The rain from heaven can bring about harvest on earth. As it rains, it does not return to the heavens, instead it waters the earth. As the earth receives the rain, it responds by bringing forth fruit. Rain is necessary to replenish the earth.

Rain is necessary for photosynthesis, the process by which plants make food to reproduce more of their kind. This is why there is drought when it hasn't rained for a period. When no rain is present and drought comes, there is a shortage of food. This forces the earth into imbalance as the water cycle is disrupted. Even though drought happens, and the earth is dry, no matter how dry it may be, it will always respond to the introduction of water.

We can use this analogy when comparing the word of God which waters the soil of our hearts. God's word is looking for a receptive and responsive heart so that it can be transformed to bring forth the fruit of His Spirit. The word of God is looking for the soil of a person's heart to water it. There are many prophetic declarations that have been released in the atmosphere, they cannot return to God void, you have to learn how to grab hold of it and believe for yourself. It can't return to God if it hasn't accomplished what it was sent to do.

**For Contemplation**

1. As a farmer tills the soil in preparation for sowing, how do you prepare your heart to receive the word and for the word to take root?

**NOTES:**

________________________________________

________________________________________

________________________________________

**Prayer changes things and people; make it a priority.**

# Day 194

***"Whatever you become is more important than who you were."***

*"Better is the end of a thing than the beginning thereof: and the patient in spirit is better than the proud in spirit. Be not hasty in thy spirit to be angry: for anger resteth in the bosom of fools. Say not thou, What is the cause that the former days were better than these? for thou dost not enquire wisely concerning this"* (Ecclesiastes 7:8-10 ).

As you become a new creature in Christ, the old man and things will remain in the past. Your past does not last. The person you become in Christ is more important than who you were outside of Christ. As the Lord has called all of us and brought us into His marvellous light. The light of God now has the power to transform us and redirect our path in Him.

Do not let your past dictate who you are now. As you come into God, remember that His grace covers a multitude of sins. These sins no longer have authority over you because, in Christ, we are now under the law of grace. Do not allow what you have done in your past to affect your service to God now. You should use it to reference where God took you from, and now you are where He has called you to be.

**For Contemplation**

1. Reflect on 2 Corinthians 5:17. Identify the newness in your life since you were born again.

**NOTES:**

____________________________________________

____________________________________________

____________________________________________

**Prayer changes things and people; make it a priority.**

# Day 195

*"Before you meet God, you are just a mere man. When you experience God, you become a living soul."*

*"And the LORD God formed man of the dust of the ground, and breathed into his nostrils the breath of life; and man became a living soul. And the LORD God planted a garden eastward in Eden; and there He put the man whom He had formed"*( Genesis 2:7-8).

The breath of God transforms man into a living soul. An experience with God brings about change. Outside of God, you are just merely existing here on earth, but once you encounter God, His Spirit now lives in you. When you encounter God, you cannot remain the same and have the same mentality you had outside of God.

In God, we now live by the Spirit and not by the flesh. We live according to the principles of God. The breath of God is in us all, it sustains us. The breath of God keeps us alive.

**For Contemplation**

1. Recall your first encounter with God, what happened?

**NOTES:**

________________________________________

________________________________________

________________________________________

**Prayer changes things and people; make it a priority.**

# Day 196

*"God, in every circumstance, give me Your peace."*

*"Be careful for nothing; but in every thing by prayer and supplication with thanksgiving let your requests be made known unto God. And the peace of God, which passeth all understanding, shall keep your hearts and minds through Christ Jesus"* (Philippians 4:6-7).

The peace of God can keep you in all situations. His peace surpasses human comprehension. In situations where the flesh will initiate a state of fear, a person living by the Spirit of God will have peace even in the midst of turmoil.

The peace of God allows you to make decisions without the interference of the flesh. Peace is not just given from God, but it is also the fruit of His Spirit. Hence, peace is an observable trait, and people should be able to see the peace of God in you. Ask God to give you peace at all times.

**For Contemplation**

1. Peace is a fruit of the spirit in every believer. It is also a spirit and an atmosphere. Be sure to utilize it everywhere you go, especially in strange places.

**NOTES:**

______________________________________________

______________________________________________

______________________________________________

**Prayer changes things and people; make it a priority.**

# Day 197

***"Satan can plan, but cannot determine the outcome of his plans. The outcome is determined by what you believe and speak."***

*"No weapon that is formed against thee shall prosper; and every tongue that shall rise against thee in judgment thou shalt condemn. This is the heritage of the servants of the Lord, and their righteousness is of me, saith the Lord"* (Isaiah 54:17).

The devil is always plotting and sending his agents against the people of God. However, the devil has no right to a life in Christ. He can make his plans against you, but the words you speak can change the outcome of his desires.

If you believe that you are a child of God and that no weapon formed against you shall prosper, then this is your birthright. You do not have to work for this; by being a child of God, as long as you speak the right words, the plans of the enemy will not affect you.

**For Contemplation**

1. Every day when praying, condemn every tongue that speaks negatively about your life. When you condemn the tongues, which are the weapons, they can't prosper.

**NOTES:**

______________________________

______________________________

______________________________

**Prayer changes things and people; make it a priority.**

# Day 198

***" If you are anointed to do something, then you can do it over and over again."***

*"But the anointing which ye have received of Him abideth in you, and ye need not that any man teach you: but as the same anointing teacheth you of all things, and is truth, and is no lie, and even as it hath taught you, ye shall abide in Him"* (1 John 2:27).

The anointing is the power of Elohim to do. This power is upon and within you. It is the potential of God being placed within you. Therefore, when you are anointed to carry out a specific task, it is now of the power of God and not from your own strength.

Once God has anointed you, the anointing abides in you. You can show forth God's glory over and over again. You need only lean on God's power and not on your own understanding.

**For Contemplation**

1. Which anointing is working in your life today to accomplish what God wants done through you?

**NOTES:**

______________________________________________

______________________________________________

______________________________________________

**Prayer changes things and people; make it a priority.**

# Day 199

***"If you can buy something that you can afford, then it is your money at work and not your faith."***

*"And the Lord shall make thee plenteous in goods, in the fruit of thy body, and in the fruit of thy cattle, and in the fruit of thy ground, in the land which the Lord sware unto thy fathers to give thee"* (Deuteronomy 28:11).

The Lord makes us have plenty, not our incomes. If it is that you have used what you have earned to purchase something, then faith was not exercised in this scenario. It was within your means of affordability. The harmful truth is that people have more trust in their income than they do in God.

People have more confidence in what they can see. Faith is not the belief in something you can see, but it is belief in the unseen, the evidence of things not seen, and "the just shall live by faith" (Hebrews 10:38).

Your faith is not the use of what you already have. It is believing in the power of God to do what seems to be impossible here on earth. Our faith should not lie in the material things we have here on earth. Our faith should not be limited to the principles that govern this world; hence, we should put our faith in the everlasting God.

**For Contemplation**

1. Think of something you need to help you to advance the kingdom of God. Pray, believe, and have faith for it every day until you receive it. Remember to share your testimony.

**NOTES:**

______________________________________________

______________________________________________

______________________________________________

**Prayer changes things and people; make it a priority.**

# Day 200

***"You may not always see God working, but you have to trust His character and know that He will come through for you."***

*"God is not a man, that He should lie; neither the son of man, that He should repent: hath He said, and shall He not do it? or hath He spoken, and shall He not make it good"* (Numbers 23:19)?

The character of God is free from flaws. He is not unreliable, nor is He forgetful. Once He says He will do something, He will. God is unlike anyone we know, He is beyond human comprehension, and is indescribable.

The Word of God cannot return to Him because it has to fulfill what it was assigned to do. Our God is an unchanging God, and once He speaks the word, it does not change. Therefore, since God is unchanging, the promises from Him cannot change. The covenant-keeping God does not forget the promises to His children.

God is a marvel to us, and our minds may not be able to fully comprehend Him in all His glory. But He chose to reveal Himself to us through His word, and even through encounters with Him. *"For by Him were all things created, that are in heaven, and that are in earth, visible and invisible, whether they be thrones, or dominions, or principalities, or powers: all things were created by Him, and for Him: And He is before all things, and by Him all things consist"* (Colossians 1:16 - 17).

Our God is self-existent. He does not require help from anyone to do anything. He existed before the reality of time even came into existence. No matter how unfaithful we may be, God remains faithful to us. It does not matter what you may see around you; you only need to trust God's heart. You have to know that He has your best interest at His heart. He will not leave you.

### For Contemplation

1. What are the characteristics of God? Do you possess any of those characteristics?

### NOTES:

______________________________________________

______________________________________________

______________________________________________

**Prayer changes things and people; make it a priority.**

# Day 201

***"The prophetic word of God has the same effect that light has on darkness."***

*"We have also a more sure word of prophecy; whereunto ye do well that ye take heed, as unto a light that shineth in a dark place, until the day dawn, and the day star arise in your hearts"* (2 Peter 1:19).

The gift of prophecy comes from God. Prophetic words should refer to the future or point towards events of the future. The word of prophecy (God), is reliable and sure. As you receive a prophetic word from God, your faith must be at the place knowing that as the words are spoken, it is done in Jesus' name.

God reveals prophetic words through men, but we can also find prophetic words over our life in His Word. The Bible has numerous promises that we can speak over our lives. The verse above says when you take heed to prophetic words and instructions, you will do well. Therefore, you can listen to the prophetic word of God, and succeed. *"This book of the law shall not depart out of thy mouth; but thou shalt meditate therein day and night, that thou mayest observe to do according to all that is written therein: for then thou shalt make thy way prosperous, and then thou shalt have good success"* (Joshua 1:8).

Meditating on the Word of God means you pause and spend time grasping the revelation of what you are reading. For some people, it can take days to spend on even one verse. As we see a cow's digestion process, which for some may be disturbing, but it gets the job done. The cow eats the food, digest it and then regurgitates the same digested food only to eat it back. As we eat the bread of Heaven, the word of God, we should spend time to know it, after which, we should repeatedly study it so that the precepts of God are embedded within us and we can share it. As we receive prophetic words, they light the pathway of life before us. As light scatters the darkness, so does the word of God. It eliminates all doubt and uncertainty.

**For Contemplation**

1. Remember when you receive prophesies to pray over them and war for them.
2. Find three Bible verses, speak them over your life, and hold God to His word.

NOTES:

______________________________________________

______________________________________________

______________________________________________

**Prayer changes things and people; make it a priority.**

# Day 202

***"When it is time for anything to happen in your life, nothing can stop it."***

*"For the Lord of hosts hath purposed, and who shall disannul it? and his hand is stretched out, and who shall turn it back"*(Isaiah 14:27)?

God works with seasons and times, He does not work according to them but with them. This is important to understand because God is not limited by time. Hence, God does work if the timing is right. He works according to His will and desire, which can be portrayed throughout different seasons.

Have you ever noticed that some months are more fruitful for you than others? This doesn't mean that God takes a break. It means that God works in different seasons, which helps to exercise our discernment of times and seasons. This helps us to know why and how to pray during specific months of the year, which prevents us from experiencing recurring negative cycles in our lives and generations.

No one can stop God's work in your life; no one can curse someone God has already blessed (Numbers 23:20). Time responds to God's move; He does not respond to time; He controls it. Your life is in the hands of the Creator; no one can affect it.

## For Contemplation

1. Analyse your life, which months or seasons are the most fruitful for you or give you the most testimonies.

NOTES:

---

---

---

**Prayer changes things and people; make it a priority.**

# Day 203

***"Sheep can hardly recognize wolves, only the shepherd can see them and save the sheep."***

*"Beware of false prophets, which come to you in sheep's clothing, but inwardly they are ravening wolves"* (Matthew 7:15).

The Spirit of God inside you should control your very senses. God controls your physical senses through the spirit of discernment. As Christians, we must depend on God to reveal things that are hidden to us. Pastors and leaders in the church should be good shepherds to the flock they are set to watch. They are supposed to look, smell, sound, and behave like what God ordained them to be. Their characteristics should be easily identifiable to the sheep they protect.

The good shepherd protects the flock from external forces that will try to scatter them and prey upon them. Your leaders watch for your soul. Hence, you must pray for them and love them as they are held accountable to God for you. They should be happy when they speak or think of you, they should not be grieved. You are to follow your leader as they follow Christ.

**For Contemplation**

1. Pray that God increases your discernment and that of your leaders to know the wolves as they come.

NOTES:

________________________________________

________________________________________

________________________________________

**Prayer changes things and people; make it a priority.**

# Day 204

***"Sometimes we stick to what we know, rather than search for hidden truths."***

*"The heart of the prudent getteth knowledge; and the ear of the wise seeketh knowledge"* (Proverbs 18:15).

As you get knowledge from God, you should desire to increase in knowledge and wisdom. As children of God, we should walk in Godly wisdom. His knowledge is the basis and foundation of the world. No matter how hard scientists try to prove another way to create the world and life, God is the only truth from which all other theories stem.

We should not be complacent with the level we are at in the knowledge of God. He is infinite, therefore, there is always something more to our Creator. We simply cannot fathom Him; but the more you seek Him, the more He reveals hidden mysteries, secrets and treasures. It is up to us to desire this, if we desire it, He will lead us to more.

### For Contemplation

1. Spend 30 minutes each day this week learning something new about God. Whether it is through a teaching from a man of God or through the word of God.

NOTES:

---

---

---

**Prayer changes things and people; make it a priority.**

# Day 205

*"The Blood of the Lamb is the symbol of protection."*

*"'And the blood shall be to you for a token upon the houses where ye are: and when I see the blood, I will pass over you, and the plague shall not be upon you to destroy you, when I smite the land of Egypt"* (Exodus 12:13).

The Blood has supernatural abilities. In the Old Testament, before the sacrifice of Jesus, we recognize that blood was a very important symbol in the lives of the Israelites. For the people's sins to be cleansed by God, each person had to take an animal to be their sacrifice. The priest will then take this animal and slaughter it, sprinkling its blood on the mercy seat of the ark of the covenant. In response to this, God would cleanse the sins of the people.

The blood was a symbol of protection. The blood was put on the doorposts of the houses of the Israelites, so that when the Spirit of the Lord passed through the land of Egypt, the lives of the firstborn would be saved. As we see the Old Testament unfolding in the New Testament, and the New Testament unfolding now before our very eyes, Blood remains an important symbol. However, this Blood was not just blood from an animal, but from the ultimate sacrifice. We are no longer required to kill an animal for protection or for the remission of our sins because Jesus has paid that price.

The blood of Jesus is so powerful that it covers even an entire generation. Once we come to know Him, accept and confess Him as Lord, the Blood of Jesus now speaks for us and our bloodline. As we are marked with His blood, we can assure ourselves that no weapon formed against us shall prosper, whether it be physical danger, spiritual danger, sickness or disease. The blood of Jesus covers and we are saved through grace.

**For Contemplation**

1. Compare the stories of Moses putting the blood on the door and Christians utilizing the blood of Jesus. What similarities have you found?

**NOTES:**

________________________________________

________________________________________

________________________________________

**Prayer changes things and people; make it a priority.**

# Day 206

***"If you want the best of anything in life, you have to work consistently for it."***

*"Those things, which ye have both learned, and received, and heard, and seen in me, do: and the God of peace shall be with you"*(Philippians 4:9).

Your grandparents or parents may have said to you, "Practice makes perfect." In this case, if you want to achieve what you desire, you must first change the mindset you have and believe that you have received what you desired, while you practise diligently. As you think you have received it, you must behave like it.

Your thoughts are powerful, because from your thoughts actions are birthed accordingly. Actions are not random, they are purposeful and are intended to achieve a specific goal. Practice aligning your thoughts and speech to what you want to see because, as a man thinks, so is he (Proverbs 23:7). The thoughts you have had, shaped you into the person you are today. Renew your mind daily with the word of God, speak the word of God, even before physically attaining it. Your confessions and actions should not change because you haven't seen the manifestations yet.

**For Contemplation**

1. Think of what you want to happen over the next three days. Pray, align your thoughts and speech, then watch what happens. Be sure to share your testimony.

**NOTES:**

---

---

---

**Prayer changes things and people; make it a priority.**

# Day 207

***"When God gives you a passion for something, He also gives you the grace for it."***

*"And whatsoever ye do in word or deed, do all in the name of the Lord Jesus, giving thanks to God and the Father by Him"*(Colossians 3:17).

Your desires in life should be fueled by the Spirit of God inside of you. Hence, your godly desires will be sustained by Him.

Anything that you have a burning desire to change is your purpose, and God will equip you to ensure this change happens. Wherever your heart is, there also lies your treasure (Matthew 6:21). Your heart searches for what it desires but doesn't have yet. Your purpose causes you to make a difference, which brings about the desired change. As you pursue your purpose, God will equip you with the things you need both physically and spiritually to ensure you fulfill His will in your life.

**For Contemplation**

1. What is your passion? Pray that God increases the grace on your life to carry out this passion.

**NOTES:**

________________________________________

________________________________________

________________________________________

**Prayer changes things and people; make it a priority.**

# Day 208

***"Giving is an opportunity for restoration to come to your family."***

*"Bring ye all the tithes into the storehouse, that there may be meat in mine house, and prove me now herewith, saith the Lord of hosts, if I will not open you the windows of heaven, and pour you out a blessing, that there shall not be room enough to receive it. And I will rebuke the devourer for your sakes, and he shall not destroy the fruits of your ground; neither shall your vine cast her fruit before the time in the field, saith the Lord of hosts"* (Malachi 3:10-11).

Giving to the Lord what He requires from us results in the Lord rewarding us. Your giving has the power to break the spirit of robbery, poverty and lack from your life. Praying is not the only solution to this problem, you must abide by the Word of God, by giving.

You have to give your way out of poverty. This counteracts the doubt that comes with this spirit. This doubt prevents you from believing that God can provide for you and sustain you. When you release your gift unto the Lord, you are also releasing faith which attracts God to you. As you give unto Him, He will restore all that was taken from you and give you more.

**For Contemplation**

1. Each time you give a gift, give it an assignment. Speak to it and be expectant of the manifestations.

**NOTES:**

______________________________________________

______________________________________________

______________________________________________

**Prayer changes things and people; make it a priority.**

# Day 209

***"According to the context by which you work, your reward will be given."***

*"For he that soweth to his flesh shall of the flesh reap corruption; but he that soweth to the Spirit shall of the Spirit reap life everlasting. And let us not be weary in well doing: for in due season we shall reap, if we faint not"*(Galatians 6:8-9.

The manner in which you work, is the same manner in which you will reap the consequences. If you work in the flesh, your result will be that of the flesh. But if you work in the spirit, you will reap the rewards by the Spirit. As you work, the Bible says do it heartily as unto God (Colossians 3:23). This means that even at your secular job, as a child of God, the work you do in society must be done as you would do anything unto the Lord. As you add and benefit the society, you should still be led by the Spirit.

You must exemplify honesty, diligence, integrity on your job, and wherever you go. The rewards of the Lord are sure and He will not withhold anything good from you.

**For Contemplation**

1. Analyse your role in your place of work. Are your attitude and efforts pleasing to God? Can your coworkers see God in you?

**NOTES:**

__________________________________________________

__________________________________________________

__________________________________________________

**Prayer changes things and people; make it a priority.**

# Day 210

***"Be kind to every person you meet, you may never know who they will turn out to be."***

*"And be ye kind one to another, tenderhearted, forgiving one another, even as God for Christ's sake hath forgiven you"* (Ephesians 4:32).

Being kind is not specific to a certain group of people, you should be kind to everybody. It is hard to be kind to certain people, especially if they may be difficult to deal with. However, this is no justification for you to treat people poorly.

Throughout the Bible, especially in the New Testament, we see scriptures telling us to be kind and loving towards others, even our enemies. This shows that God is interested in how we treat each other. We must remember that everyone we see is God's creation and He loves them. Therefore, we are only expected to love them as well.

*"If it be possible, as much as lieth in you, live peaceably with all men"* (Romans 12:18). We should try to live peaceably with all men. The Bible did not specify any group, but said all men. It is important that we ensure that our hearts remain pure, we cannot be so deep in our own mindset, that the basic principles of our Christianity are being side-stepped. Only the pure in heart shall see God (Matthew 5:8). Pure means being synonymous with the character of God. God doesn't treat us as we deserve, so why do we think we have the right above God? Some people in life will do things that hurt us, but for our soul's sake, forgive and love them. It doesn't make sense that you are kind to some people, maybe because they are in esteemed positions. This is not real kindness. We have to learn how to love without a motive. We can only do that when we know God and experience His love. Love God, live good and be kind.

**For Contemplation**

1. When people ill-treat you, make it your duty to be extra kind to them.

**NOTES:**

________________________________________________

________________________________________________

________________________________________________

**Prayer changes things and people; make it a priority.**

# Day 211

***"When persons are unproductive in church, they will be cut off."***

*"And now also the axe is laid unto the root of the trees: every tree therefore which bringeth not forth good fruit is hewn down, and cast into the fire"* (Luke 3:9).

In the natural world, if a tree is not bearing fruit; it is not pruned but cut down. This is so because the tree hasn't produced any fruit and it is not carrying out its purpose.

We see this analogy being used to explain the fate of fruitless Christians. In this scripture, John is warning the people of God about impending judgement. He was preparing for the coming of the Messiah. This analogy does not mean that you will be removed from the body of Christ, but if you are not producing the fruit of God's Spirit, then this means that you are not truly rooted and grounded. If you are not rooted and grounded, then the devices of the devil will distract you so much that you wander from the presence of God. You become so entangled with the lust of the flesh, the lust of the eyes, and the pride of life that the production of spiritual fruit is thwarted, and you wither.

*"I am the vine, ye are the branches: He that abideth in me, and I in him, the same bringeth forth much fruit: for without me ye can do nothing. If a man abide not in me, he is cast forth as a branch, and is withered; and men gather them, and cast them into the fire, and they are burned"* (John 15:5-6 ).

Only if you connect yourself to the true vine will you produce godly fruit. The more you produce godly fruit, the more you are being saturated in the presence of God and being transformed daily by His word.

**For Contemplation**

1. Are you a fruitless tree? What fruits have you produced?

**NOTES:**

________________________________________

________________________________________

________________________________________

**Prayer changes things and people; make it a priority.**

# Day 212

***"Christianity is not just a word-based religion, it is also an evidence-based religion."***

*"For the kingdom of God is not in word, but in power"* (1 Corinthians 4:20).

Saying you are part of the Kingdom is good, but ensure that your actions show that you are truly a part of His Kingdom. People should see that you are a child of God. The signs that follow you should point others to the power of God, and the fruits that come from you should point them towards the love of God.

*"My little children, let us not love in word, neither in tongue; but in deed and in truth"* (1 John 3:18). Our love towards others should not be lip-service, but it must be seen through our actions and stem from the place of truth, which is in God. You cannot truly love until you know God, who is love.

### For Contemplation

1. Picture yourself through the eyes of your least favorite family member or coworker. Are you seeing a child of God? Why or why not?

### NOTES:

________________________________________

________________________________________

________________________________________

**Prayer changes things and people; make it a priority.**

# Day 213

***"When people forsake you, then God will take you and bring you to the next level."***

*"When my father and my mother forsake me, then the Lord will take me up"* (Psalm 27:10).

The Lord will take you into His arms when others forsake you. The Lord is gracious and compassionate towards us, even when we were sinners, He sent His only Son to die for us. This shows the heart of God towards us, despite what we even do to Him.

People may choose to forsake you for various reasons, but God does not leave you. He has promised us in His word, which can never return to Him void. As God takes you in, He will carry you through and bring you into a better state. He will not just be there with you in your desolate times, He will rebuild you and transform you.

### For Contemplation

1. The Lord will never leave you nor forsake you, He is a very present help in trouble.

**NOTES:**

________________________________________

________________________________________

________________________________________

**Prayer changes things and people; make it a priority.**

# Day 214

***"You can be living pure and holy before God, but be aware of open doors that the devil and his agents can access."***

*"Lest Satan should get an advantage of us: for we are not ignorant of his devices"* (2 Corinthians 2:11).

Do not be ignorant of the devil's devices. Do not think that because you are living pure and holy, that the devil will not try to attack you. He is always on the lookout to see if he can accuse you of doing something before God. He is a "news carrier", and he seeks to defame your character in God.

To every man there are gates, which are entry points to a man's soul. We should be careful when these gates are opened and to whom they are opened. In the story of Job, the devil was going to and fro in the earth, until he found himself before the Lord. This means the devil has been accessing portals until he reached before God. The devil was given the opportunity by God to affect Job. However, Job did not curse God for all the misfortune that the devil caused him.

When the devil comes, you get rid of him by resisting him (James 4:7). Resist the devil's temptations, and his plans will be destroyed. You may plead the blood of Jesus, but the Bible did not tell us this is how you get rid of the devil. You may say that you are always in the presence of God, but remember that Satan entered Judas, who was physically in the presence of Jesus. You have to resist him, and he will flee.

**For Contemplation**

1. Meditate on Matthew 4: 1 -11. Take note of how Jesus resisted Satan each time.

**NOTES:**

________________________________________

________________________________________

________________________________________

**Prayer changes things and people; make it a priority.**

# Day 215

*"There is power in agreement."*

*"Again, I say unto you, that if two of you shall agree on earth as touching anything that they shall ask, it shall be done for them of my Father which is in heaven"* (Matthew 18:19).

Man was created out of agreement. God said, "Let us make man in our image." He was speaking to someone and letting them know what He wanted to do. Here, we see the importance of agreement.

Agreeing means you are of the same mind, there is no ambiguity or confusion, and agreement keeps you aligned with what was spoken, whether good or evil. Jesus says if two agree here on earth, it shall be done once they ask. This is the assurance we have when we agree and seal it in Jesus' name.

Once there is agreement, God can destroy Satan's plans. You have to agree with God's word if you want to see God's promises in your life.

**For Contemplation**

1. In your Bible, find examples of the power of agreement.

**NOTES:**

________________________________________

________________________________________

________________________________________

**Prayer changes things and people; make it a priority.**

# Day 216

*When there is a shift in the 'cosmos' or in the world, God is up to something."*

*"The heavens declare the glory of God; and the firmament sheweth his handywork"* (Psalm 19:1).

Nature is an expression of God's glory. It reveals God's nature. God can use nature's systems to reveal when He is angry, when He wants to speak, or even when He wants to give us direction.

We can discern when God wants to get our attention when there is a change in nature. In the days of Noah, God chose to use water to destroy the earth because of the overwhelming sin of man. He really wanted to give the earth a good cleanse. Even though God is merciful, this doesn't mean we should cross the line with Him, we must remember He is a righteous judge by nature. God sent warnings before He sent the flood. He even gave them time to repent, but the hardening of the heart can prevent us from obtaining mercy from God. Our Lord is merciful, that He sent warnings before He sent the judgement and He told them what to do in order to stop this judgement from befalling them. But they didn't listen.

After He sent the flood, God also used another emblem of nature to promise that He would not destroy the earth with water again. This promise applies to us now. Whenever you see the rainbow in the sky, remember that God is a promise-keeping God, the covenant-keeping God. Therefore, every promise He has for you will be granted to you.

**For Contemplation**

1. Read the story of the flood. What happened after the flood?

**NOTES:**

______________________________________________

______________________________________________

______________________________________________

**Prayer changes things and people; make it a priority.**

# Day 217

***"Do not be limited by your incapabilities, but look for the possibilities."***

*"I can do all things through Christ which strengtheneth me"* (Philippians 4:13 ).

Do not be discouraged by what you think you cannot do. You are living through the Spirit of God. The same power that resurrected Jesus from the dead is inside of you. You have to remember nothing is impossible with God. As He lives in you, you are not bound by what your physical body can do.

The verse says you can do all through Christ. It is interesting that Christ was used in this verse. We normally see the word "Christ" following Jesus, and we call Him Jesus Christ. But the word Christ, is a title and it means 'the Anointed One'. Jesus is the anointed One from God and He lives in you. Therefore, if you have the 'anointed One' in you, it means that you are now also anointed to do what you thought impossible. He gives you strength, even when you are physically weak.

**For Contemplation**

1. Share a testimony about how God strengthened you to do what you thought you could not.

**NOTES:**

______________________________________________

______________________________________________

______________________________________________

**Prayer changes things and people; make it a priority.**

# Day 218

***"When a curse comes upon a thing, it affects the quality of that life."***

*"Moreover, all these curses shall come upon thee, and shall pursue thee, and overtake thee, till thou be destroyed; because thou hearkenedst not unto the voice of the Lord thy God, to keep His commandments and His statutes which He commanded thee: And they shall be upon thee for a sign and for a wonder, and upon thy seed forever. Because thou servedst not the Lord thy God with joyfulness, and with gladness of heart, for the abundance of all things"* (Deuteronomy 28:45-47).

Curses are declarations released over someone that affects their quality of life negatively. A curse also affects the quantity of life and life cycle of a thing. We see in Mark 11, that Jesus cursed the fig tree, resulting in it not producing fruit and withering. Curses are released by chantings using divination, however, there are also instances when God curses people. Curses are solemn utterances, intended to invoke a supernatural power that inflicts harm/punishment on someone or something.

The effects of a curse can affect an entire generation. These are known as generational curses and run through specific bloodlines. Curses can cause you to lose that which is rightfully yours. It can even fall on the innocent, as we remember Noah cursed Canaan instead of his son who was the one who dishonoured him.

Curses are effective in a generation because they have departed from the ways of God. In the absence of God the enemy can have access. These curses can be broken when someone in the family becomes the restorer of the breach. Someone has to return to God, and be the medium for deliverance.

**For Contemplation**

1. Live holy and righteous, for a curse cannot land without a cause. Let there be no cause found among you (Proverbs 26:2).

**NOTES:**

______________________________________________

______________________________________________

______________________________________________

**Prayer changes things and people; make it a priority.**

# Day 219

***"Magnifying God helps to keep pride away."***

*"I will bless the Lord at all times: His praise shall continually be in my mouth. My soul shall make her boast in the Lord: the humble shall hear thereof, and be glad. O magnify the Lord with me, and let us exalt His name together"* (Psalm 34:1-3 ).

We should boast in the Lord and not of ourselves. When we remember to magnify the Lord, we remain focused on Him. He becomes big in our sight so that it is easier for us to always see Him instead of even ourselves.

When we continuously see God, the spirit of pride cannot interfere with our mindset of God. When we want to make it all about, the constant habit of magnifying God will cause us to remain in our position before God, which is humility.

**For Contemplation**

1. Have a 10-minute worship session, praising God for His goodness.

**NOTES:**

______________________________________________

______________________________________________

______________________________________________

**Prayer changes things and people; make it a priority.**

# Day 220

***"Keep your tongue, know when to speak."***

*"Be ye not as the horse, or as the mule, which have no understanding: whose mouth must be held in with bit and bridle, lest they come near unto thee"* (Psalm 32:9 ).

One of the most important keys of wisdom is knowing when to speak and when not to. As the spirit of God is in you, He will teach you when, where and what to speak. Remember words have power, and words hold information. You have to be careful what you speak. Ask God for wisdom in your speech.

**For Contemplation**

1. Words are spirits, when you speak, ensure you are sending forth spirits that will enhance your life (John 6:63).

**NOTES:**

____________________________________________

____________________________________________

**Prayer changes things and people; make it a priority.**

# Day 221

***"Before you ask God for anything, you need to know His will."***

*"Wherefore be ye not unwise, but understanding what the will of the Lord is"* (Ephesians 5:17).

Sometimes, we pray for things we think we need and desire. We should always ask, "Is this the will of God?" Does this request align with words in His Holy Scriptures?

We must pray for God's will in our lives. Our fleshly desires can often carry us away, but we must remember that our lives are for God's glory. Life is not about us but the Christ who lives in us. When we ask for things, we must know the motive behind what we ask for. We should ensure that our motives are not based on selfish desires because the things we receive from God must be used to further His Kingdom and His glory.

**For Contemplation:**

1. Seek the will of God for your life and pray for divine alignment.

**NOTES:**

______________________________________________

______________________________________________

______________________________________________

**Prayer changes things and people; make it a priority.**

# Day 222

***"Many Christians are not learning to live on Kingdom resources but learning to live on earthly resources."***

*"Then said he unto me, Fear not, Daniel: for from the first day that thou didst set thine heart to understand, and to chasten thyself before thy God, thy words were heard, and I am come for thy words. But the prince of the kingdom of Persia withstood me one and twenty days: but, lo, Michael, one of the chief princes, came to help me; and I remained there with the kings of Persia"* (Daniel 10:12-13).

The enemy can delay our answers from God, but their plans will never prevail. In Daniel 10, we see that the angel of the Lord told him that God had already sent his answer from the very first day of his fast, but the prince of the power of the air intercepted him. This is why we should pray for our angels and the battles they may encounter on our behalf. We should pray and release the word of God, as they excel in strength at the word of God. We should pray that our prayers will be evasive to the plans of the adversary. Do not give up if something seems to be delayed. Keep your faith in God, keep speaking the right words about your situation, and watch for the change you desire.

**For Contemplation:**

1. Read Daniel 10. Notice that the angel needed reinforcement. Practice releasing reinforcements for the angel bringing your answers to you.

**NOTES:**

________________________________________________

________________________________________________

________________________________________________

**Prayer changes things and people; make it a priority.**

# Day 223

***" Success is discovering and using strategies to make things work."***

*"But his delight is in the law of the Lord; and in his law doth he meditate day and night. And he shall be like a tree planted by the rivers of water, that bringeth forth his fruit in his season; his leaf also shall not wither; and whatsoever he doeth shall prosper"* (Psalm 1:2-3 ).

As you set yourself to succeed in life, it comes from a place of discipline. As you become a tree planted by God by the rivers of water, you are now connected to the source, you are connected to the Living Water.

It is crucial that you do not remove yourself from where God has planted you in Him. This is where He will give you strategies and ideas to solve problems that can be helpful to many people. You will bring forth fruit, and you will prosper.

Success is defined differently by different people. Your success is dependent on where you are in God. As you seek Him, He will add everything to you.

**For Contemplation:**

1. How do you seek God? How often do you seek Him?

**NOTES:**

---

---

---

**Prayer changes things and people; make it a priority.**

# Day 224

***"The dominion of man is expressed verbally."***

*"And out of the ground the Lord God formed every beast of the field, and every fowl of the air; and brought them unto Adam to see what he would call them: and whatsoever Adam called every living creature, that was the name thereof"* (Genesis 2:19).

God allowed Adam to call every animal by a name. God made man into a talking spirit. God created man to have dominion over the earth and over the creatures. *"And God said, Let us make man in our image, after our likeness: and let them have dominion over the fish of the sea, and over the fowl of the air, and over the cattle, and over all the earth, and over every creeping thing that creepeth upon the earth" (Genesis* 1:26).

We should recognize that we were not initially created just to be blessed by God, but to take dominion. We should be walking in dominion. God exercised Adam's dominion by allowing him to speak. The thoughts that Adam had were manifested by the words he spoke. The thoughts of man are powerful and can dominate the creatures of the Earth.

When man became a living soul, he became a miniature version of God. You are not able to talk just for the purpose of communication, but you are given the ability to rule and dominate.

**For Contemplation:**

1. Life and death is in the power of your tongue. Use right words to take dominion over every circumstance.

**NOTES:**

______________________________________________

______________________________________________

______________________________________________

**Prayer changes things and people; make it a priority.**

# Day 225

*"You are a law enforcer."*

*"Blessed are the peacemakers: for they shall be called the children of God"* (Matthew 5:9).

We are agents of God and so we are expected to enforce the will of God in our lives. We are His instruments on earth and He will use us to show His power.

As we are expected to enforce His laws, He gives us armour that we must put on to stand and quench Satan's fiery darts. He gives us protection that we can use. His armour has offensive and defensive parts, which we use to ensure that we are covered from the devil's plans.

*"Wherefore take unto you the whole armour of God, that ye may be able to withstand in the evil day, and having done all, to stand. Stand*

*therefore, having your loins girt about with truth, and having on the breastplate of righteousness; And your feet shod with the preparation of the gospel of peace; Above all, taking the shield of faith, wherewith ye shall be able to quench all the fiery darts of the wicked. And take the helmet of salvation, and the sword of the Spirit, which is the word of God:"* (Ephesians 6: 13-17).

We say we are protected from the devil, but it is not something that you just say. We need to be aware of our position in God. Darkness will always attack light, but we have our protection in the hands of God. If they touch you, they touch God. Every time we speak that does not align with what God says, we are fighting against God's will. Stand in your rightful place in God through the authority of Jesus Christ.

**For Contemplation:**

1. How do you enforce the will of God in your life?
2. Just as you clothe yourself daily, remèmber to put on the whole armour of God.

**NOTES:**

______________________________________________

______________________________________________

______________________________________________

**Prayer changes things and people; make it a priority.**

# Day 226

***"Distractions will rob you of your purpose."***

*"Now it came to pass, as they went, that He entered into a certain village: and a certain woman named Martha received Him into her house. And she had a sister called Mary, which also sat at Jesus' feet, and heard His word. But Martha was cumbered about much serving, and came to Him, and said, Lord, dost thou not care that my sister hath left me to serve alone? bid her therefore that she help me. And Jesus answered and said*

*unto her, Martha, Martha, thou art careful and troubled about many things: But one thing is needful: and Mary hath chosen that good part, which shall not be taken away from her"* (Luke 10:38-42).

Distractions can divert us from God's presence. When you are distracted, you are preoccupied, unable to concentrate, and unable to fully complete a task. Martha had Jesus in her presence; however, she was bothered by external things that were of little importance in Jesus's presence.

Distractions take our eyes off the one who is truly important. Peter became distracted by the waves that Jesus had already conquered. He took his eyes off, and this shifted his focus to seeing himself in danger instead of going straight to safety.

However, we should be like Mary; when you are in the presence of God, He should be the only focus. Ask God to block out all distractions as you spend time with Him. When you do this, then you will be completely saturated with His presence, and He will reveal Himself to you in ways you have not experienced before. The cares of life can be overwhelming, but this should not be powerful enough to make us lose sight of how powerful our God is over every situation. If you spend more time in His presence the cares of the world will fade away and all you will see is Him. Don't let your distractions become your main attraction.

**For Contemplation:**

1. When you know God's will for your life, you can easily identify distractions. Spend time finding God's blueprint for your life.

**NOTES:**

___

___

___

**Prayer changes things and people; make it a priority.**

# Day 227

***"It is easy for God to take you out of a problem, but it becomes a problem when you put yourself back into the same bondage."***

*"Stand fast therefore in the liberty wherewith Christ hath made us free, and be not entangled again with the yoke of bondage"* (Galatians 5:1).

God is a deliverer; even in very difficult situations, God will free you from the grips of evil. We must ensure that when God delivers us and frees us from a situation, we do not fall back into Satan's trap again.

We need to understand that when we get delivered, we should maintain our deliverance. We must take steps to prevent us from regressing into the same problem we overcame. Maintaining our deliverance is not just in prayer; you must also practically take steps that will help you keep moving forward and not backward. There are decisions that you will have to make that will help you keep at your place of freedom in God.

Choose to remain free in God, do not fall back into the traps of Satan.

**For Contemplation:**

1. Read Luke 11: 21 – 26, and notice that Jesus Himself says the last state of that man is worse than the first. Make it a priority to maintain your deliverance.

**NOTES:**

______________________________________________

______________________________________________

______________________________________________

**Prayer changes things and people; make it a priority.**

# Day 228

***"People involved in anything negative can potentially open doors that affect your life and destiny."***

*"Can two walk together, except they be agreed"* (Amos 3:3)?

If you associate yourself with people who have open doors, if you are not spiritually aware and know how to guard yourself, then you can be affected. If you associate with someone, that means at some point you will have to agree with them. Therefore, spiritually, they connect with you, and a transfer of spirits can take place.

Always remember to ask God to protect you as you go out and to increase your discernment so that you will know with whom to associate.

**For Contemplation:**

1. Pray for the people with whom you interact daily. Guard your life and don't let anyone enter that should not.

**NOTES:**

______________________________________________

______________________________________________

______________________________________________

**Prayer changes things and people; make it a priority.**

# Day 229

***" God can never do anything for a family without an intercessor."***

*"And Samuel said, Gather all Israel to Mizpeh, and I will*

*pray for you unto the Lord"* (1 Samuel 7:5).

God can use someone to be the doorway of restoration for a family or nation. Samuel was the restorer of the breach in the scripture. The children of Israel were drawn away from God by their sins. They were serving other idols, and their sin was before the Lord. Samuel was sent to warn them that if they did not repent, God would deliver them into the hands of the Philistines. Then Samuel interceded for Israel before the Lord and made a sacrifice unto Him.

The Philistines were now planning to attack the children of Israel as they were gathered in Mizpeh, but Samuel continued to make petitions to the Lord for them, and He heard and delivered them from their enemies.

God can use you to restore your family and generation. He must trust that you will keep His statutes and laws in your generation. He expects you to teach your generation His principles. When you live for God, you become His standard.

**For Contemplation:**

1. Be an intercessor for your family. Pray for them, their destinies, and their salvation as often as possible.

**NOTES:**

---

---

---

**Prayer changes things and people; make it a priority.**

# Day 230

***"When you receive your blessings, persecution will come."***

*"And ye shall be hated of all men for my name's sake: but he that endureth to the end shall be saved"* ( Matthew 10:22 ).

Seeking God's kingdom first causes everything you need on earth to be added to you. As you receive your blessings, then persecution will come. The devil will cause persecution to come in many forms, but you must be ready and prepared to stand against it.

Do not allow persecution to run you out of your position. Your position in God should be firm and not easily removed. Do not remove yourself because of what happens in life. God is looking for someone who is already positioned.

**For Contemplation:**

1. Pray for five minutes that persecution will not run you out of your position.

**NOTES:**

______________________________________________________________

______________________________________________________________

______________________________________________________________

**Prayer changes things and people; make it a priority.**

# Day 231

***" Isaac's blessing came after he prayed for his enemies."***

*"And Isaac said unto them, Wherefore come ye to me, seeing ye hate me, and have sent me away from you? And they said, We saw certainly that the Lord was with thee: and we said, Let there be now an oath betwixt us, even betwixt us and thee, and let us make a covenant with thee; That thou wilt do us no hurt, as we have not touched thee, and as we have done unto thee nothing but good, and have sent thee away in peace: thou art now the blessed of the Lord. And he made them a feast, and they did eat and drink. And they rose up betimes in the morning, and sware one to another: and Isaac sent them away, and they departed from him in peace. And it*

*came to pass the same day, that Isaac's servants came, and told him concerning the well which they had digged, and said unto him, We have found water. And he called it Shebah: therefore the name of the city is Beersheba unto this day"(* Genesis 26:27-33).

Isaac was in a land that was unknown to him, and he was surrounded by people he did not know. These people did not like him and were very aggressive towards him. However, in the scripture, we see that Isaac's enemy came to him in peace.

Here, Isaac teaches us how to treat our enemies; he did not reject them, chase them away, or hurt them. Instead, he met with them, ate with them, and blessed them on their way. Isaac chose the opportunity to be mature in the presence of his enemies. He really overcame evil with good (Romans 12:21), he acted in a way that God would be pleased. We should love our enemies, not hate them. After he did this, water was found in the well he dug on the same day. In the same day that Isaac prayed for his enemies he received his blessings.

**For Contemplation:**

1. When you pray, pray for those who love you and also for those who despise you. Pray for their souls and salvation.

**NOTES:**

______________________________________________

______________________________________________

______________________________________________

**Prayer changes things and people; make it a priority.**

# Day 232

***"Great leaders go through great difficulties."***

*"But he that knew not, and did commit things worthy of stripes, shall be beaten with few stripes. For unto whomsoever much is given, of him shall*

*be much required: and to whom men have committed much, of him they will ask the more"*(Luke 12:48).

If you desire to be a great leader, you must be prepared to face difficult situations. These situations strengthen you and deepen your character in God; they do not destroy you.

These situations force you to become selfless, a quality of a great leader. As a leader, you are responsible for leading others and facilitating their going even further than you have.

Every leader uses a bad experience or a mistake as a stepping stone towards an extraordinary destination. Leaders should not be ashamed of their past because God allows them to go through these situations so that they can tell others that God can do it for them too. Problems produce leaders; the God factor makes great leaders. God's potential takes you to a different level, and God's destiny completes you.

**For Contemplation:**

1. Are you called to be a leader? Why or why not?
2. What good or bad experiences have you had that you can use as a lesson for others?

**NOTES:**

---

---

---

**Prayer changes things and people; make it a priority.**

# Day 233

---

***"God will have mercy on whom He chooses."***

---

*"For He saith to Moses, I will have mercy on whom I will have mercy, and I will have compassion on whom I will have compassion"*( Romans 9:15).

Some people are chosen by God specifically. These people are divinely protected and blessed. He chooses whom He will grant mercy and compassion.

**For Contemplation:**

1. Share a testimony of how God has been merciful to you.

**NOTES:**

________________________________________

________________________________________

________________________________________

**Prayer changes things and people; make it a priority.**

# Day 234

***"Principalities set the tone over countries."***

*"The kings of the earth set themselves, and the rulers take counsel together, against the Lord, and against his anointed, saying, Let us break their bands asunder, and cast away their cords from us. He that sitteth in the heavens shall laugh: the Lord shall have them in derision"*(Psalm 2:2-4).

Principality is the name given to a rank; they are not necessarily spirits. There are good and evil principalities and there are certain spirits that operate in the rank of principality. Some spirits are set over countries, and they can only operate within the designated boundary. These are called territorial spirits. These spirits are set over the nation based on their stance. If they are for God, then there are good principalities ruling over the land. If the nation is plunged into wickedness by its leader, who legally gave rights to demonic principalities to rule, then the country is ruled by evil principalities.

**For Contemplation:**

1. How do you pray against evil principalities? How do you utilize good principalities?

**NOTES:**

---

---

---

**Prayer changes things and people; make it a priority.**

# Day 235

---

***"Appreciate who GOD is."***

---

*"Praise ye the Lord. O give thanks unto the Lord; for He is good: for His mercy endureth forever"*( Psalm 106:1).

Learn to appreciate who God is, not just for what He has done for you. We must love God for Himself and not for what we can get from Him. He is too precious for us to take Him for granted. Learn to honour God even before and after He does something.

**For Contemplation:**

1. Who is God to you? How do you honour God?

**NOTES:**

---

---

---

**Prayer changes things and people; make it a priority.**

# Day 236

---

***"Don't hate your problems, they remind you that you need God."***

---

*"I sought the Lord, and he heard me, and delivered me from all my fears"* (Psalm 34:4).

The Lord will deliver you from all your problems. However, we should not hate what we go through. We should remember that everything we go through is part of a bigger picture that we are not yet seeing.

When you go through your problems, they remind you that you must always depend on God. They bring you to the place of seeking God. Let us be honest: If we did not encounter some difficult situations, we would not have sought God. You needed help. Your struggles help you remain at Jesus's feet.

Do not worry He will deliver you from every fear.

**For Contemplation:**

1. What fears do you need deliverance from? Leave them at the foot of the cross.

**NOTES:**

______________________________________________

______________________________________________

______________________________________________

**Prayer changes things and people; make it a priority.**

# Day 237

***" One of the most forgotten elements of the armour of God, is the gospel of peace."***

*"And your feet shod with the preparation of the gospel of peace"* (Ephesians 6:15).

We must never forget how we got saved. We should never forget the agony that Jesus went through for our sins. We should never forget the importance of the gospel. The Gospel of peace is a part of the armour of God, which is a necessary adornment for us Christians. Our feet should be shod with the preparation of the gospel of peace. Our feet take us to where we want to go or need to go. Therefore, as you put on the gospel of peace on your feet, it means that wherever you go, you must walk with the gospel. Wherever you go as you have the gospel, you should share this gospel with everyone you meet. We are instructed to preach the gospel in and out of season (2 Timothy 4:2). The gospel of Jesus should always be in our conversations.

*"And He said unto them, Go ye into all the world, and preach the gospel to every creature"* (Mark 16:15). Jesus commands us to go into the world and preach the gospel to every living creature. If you are a part of the Kingdom of God, you are not expected to only be in church and not evangelize to those who are lost. It is wise when we win souls for the Kingdom of God, and He wants us to share the life-changing good news with others. Ask God to give you boldness and the right words when you share His good news. When you bring the gospel with power, you won't need to argue. You are not the one who saves the person, but you are the facilitator who carries the news to them, after which the Holy Spirit will now work on the individual's heart.

Remember, God calls you to go into the world to preach the good news of salvation.

**For Contemplation:**

1. Since you have been saved, have you told anyone about Jesus? How many souls have you led to the Lord?

**NOTES:**

______________________________

______________________________

______________________________

**Prayer changes things and people; make it a priority.**

# Day 238

---

***"God has an agenda, but so does the devil."***

---

*"And the Lord said unto Satan, From whence comest thou? And Satan answered the Lord, and said, From going to and fro in the earth, and from walking up and down in it"* (Job 2:2).

The devil has an agenda, if he is going to and from about the earth, he is not just aimlessly walking the earth. He is on a mission. *"Be sober, be vigilant; because your adversary the devil, as a roaring lion, walketh about, seeking whom he may devour"*(1 Peter 5:8).

The devil is going about the earth, seeking whom he may devour. This means that it is not guaranteed to the devil that he can devour anyone, this can only happen if he is presented with the opportunity. The person has to be the one who allows themself to be susceptible to the devil's devices. The devil wants to distract you from God, and he wants to draw people away from God. Therefore, he will use the enticing things of the world to influence the flesh. His agenda is contrary to the will of God. He has agents that carry out his evil doings on the earth because he is not omnipresent, therefore, he needs help to get his job done. These agents are not only the fallen angels, but the devil has men under his control who are destined to distract others into the trap of Satan.

There are game shows, secular artistes, provocative movies, talk shows, and even sports are forms of distractions that the devil uses. He uses them to distract the hearts of men so that they fall into vanity as they give in to the lust of their flesh. We should be aware of these devices and not be distracted and drawn away as others are. The devil is always roaming. Ensure that you and your family are strong in the Lord and clothed in God's armour to stand against his devices.

**For Contemplation:**

1. The devil cannot kill everyone; from some, he will steal and some, he will destroy. Be not ignorant of his devices, live a righteous life.
2. Spend five minutes praying against the devices of the enemy, especially those you recognise in your life.

NOTES:

---

**Prayer changes things and people; make it a priority.**

# Day 239

***" Boast about God even in your sufferings."***

*"My soul shall make her boast in the Lord: the humble shall hear thereof, and be glad"* (Psalm 34:2).

Boasting in the Lord eliminates the desire to boast about yourself. God is the one who deserves the praise, not you. You are simply a vessel through which He reveals His glory so that others can see and also come to know Him. The events in your life should bring glory to God.

As you boast in God, you allow others to hear of how great God is. As you tell them more about Him and His power, they will be encouraged because your testimony gives them hope. As they have this hope, along with their faith in God, they are assured that God will also come through for them. We should tell of His excellent greatness, even amid troubles; God is keeping you alive, and that is something for which to give Him thanks.

**For Contemplation:**

1. Today, tell five persons of the goodness of God. You can share testimonies of persons in the Bible or your own blessing.

NOTES:

---

**Prayer changes things and people; make it a priority.**

# Day 240

***"The trials you go through are not meant to harm you, but to purify you."***

*"My brethren, count it all joy when ye fall into divers temptations; Knowing this, that the trying of your faith worketh patience. But let patience have her perfect work, that ye may be perfect and entire, wanting nothing"* (James 1: 2-4 ).

The trials we experience should not overwhelm us to the point of despair. However, they are a time for us to see ourselves more clearly as we are being purified. The trials allow us to see the true nature of our hearts.

These experiences are meant to work something in us that will allow us to be more deeply rooted in God. As we experience difficult situations, we should not miss the lesson that comes with them. Yes, we should have faith, but we should also be patient. As you wait on God, He will renew your strength. Then, you will be able to soar above your problems.

**For Contemplation:**

1. In every situation, look at how it has developed your character, how it has purified and changed you for the better.

**NOTES:**

______________________________

______________________________

______________________________

**Prayer changes things and people; make it a priority.**

# Day 241

***" Be vigilant and monitor your life, check what comes in and what goes out."***

*"Keep thy heart with all diligence; for out of it are the issues of life"* (Proverbs 4:23).

What comes out of your heart indicates what is going in there. Whatever you allow to enter into your spirit will eventually enter your heart; and whatever you allow to enter your flesh will get into your heart. You are responsible for knowing what is entering; is it something to benefit your spirit or to satisfy the flesh?

The heart reveals a person's nature, even in their subtle actions. If you are constantly feeding your flesh, then the things that exit the heart will be a result of your flesh. Ensure that the things you allow to enter will benefit your spirit and not your flesh.

**For Contemplation:**

1. Search your heart; search it through your thoughts, actions, conversations, and hobbies. Are they all pleasing to God? If not, spend time cleansing your heart and guarding it with all diligence.

**NOTES:**

______________________________________________

______________________________________________

______________________________________________

**Prayer changes things and people; make it a priority.**

# Day 242

***" When you tithe, you are tithing for your generation."***

*"Thy Kingdom come, Thy will be done on earth, as it is in heaven"* (Matthew 6:10).

*"And as I may so say, Levi also, who receiveth tithes, paid tithes in*

*Abraham. For he was yet in the loins of his father when Melchisedec met him"* (Hebrews 7:9-10).

We should honour God with our finances. As we honour God, He will reward us and secure our generation in Him. The scripture says Levi paid tithes in Abraham. Levi was Abraham's grandson and at the time of Abraham meeting with Melchisedec, Levi was not yet born. This scripture proves that you were born with your seed in you. They are then manifested when you join with the other part of their DNA, which is within the person of the opposite sex with whom you will join. Every male was born with their seed, they have the DNA of their future children within them. The same goes for females, they were born with their eggs.

Therefore, what you do now can affect the lives of your unborn children. You have to make decisions that will cause you and your family to remain in the right standing with God. As you pay your tithes the Lord will rebuke your devourer (Malachi 3:10-11). As you honour God with your tithes, he will honour His promises to you and your generation.

**For Contemplation:**

1. Spend some time repenting for your sins, transgressions, and your generation's sins. As you go forward, live a life that will benefit your generation to come.

**NOTES:**

________________________________________

________________________________________

________________________________________

**Prayer changes things and people; make it a priority.**

# Day 243

***" The one who always has his hands out to receive will always be in need."***

*the weak, and to remember the words of the Lord Jesus, how He said, It is more blessed to give than to receive"* (Acts 20:35).

If you constantly seek to receive, you will always need something. There is a blessing in giving, not when you receive. When you give, you will receive. If you constantly want to receive, then you are only thinking about yourself and not how you can be a blessing to others. Giving leans more towards the character of God, than receiving. God loved, and so He gave. We must remember that when we seek the kingdom of God instead of getting things for ourselves, God will add unto us, even that which we didn't know we needed.

Focus more on giving. Give to God, give to your neighbours, give to the poor. When you give to the poor, you become a lender to God (Proverbs 19:17). If you lend something to someone, you expect them to give it back. Therefore, as you give willingly, God will give back to you good measure, press down, shaken together and running over.

**For Contemplation:**

1. Reflect on Mathew 6:1.

**NOTES:**

___

___

___

**Prayer changes things and people; make it a priority.**

# Day 244

***"Spiritually leavening agents are bad for your spiritual health."***

*"Purge out therefore the old leaven, that ye may be a new lump, as ye are unleavened. For even Christ our Passover is sacrificed for us: Therefore*

*let us keep the feast, not with old leaven, neither with the leaven of malice and wickedness; but with the unleavened bread of sincerity and truth"* ( *1* Corinthians 5:7-8).

Leavening agents are used in cooking to make something bigger than what it naturally is, for example, in the making of bread. Before the bread is placed in the oven it is relatively flat. However, when it goes into the oven and is being transformed by the heat, the added leavening agents cause the bread to rise and get bigger.

As it relates to our spiritual lives, we should not be raised by added leavening agents, but we should only be transformed by the Spirit of God. We are encouraged to purge ourselves from the leavening agents that can cause them to seem big but really there is nothing behind it. We were created as unleavened beings, because Jesus was our Passover. Therefore, as we are made into His image, we are also without leavening agents. We should be free from the things that will cause us to be puffed up, for instance pride.

Let go of the things that will cause you to be something you are not supposed to be. Let go of the malice and strife and be the chosen people God called you to be.

**For Contemplation:**

1. Live a life free of sin, if you currently have any sinful thoughts or ways sincerely repent and turn away from them.

**NOTES:**

________________________________________

________________________________________

________________________________________

**Prayer changes things and people; make it a priority.**

# Day 245

*" Pain can lead you to your next destination."*

*"But the God of all grace, who hath called us unto His eternal glory by Christ Jesus, after that ye have suffered a while, make you perfect, stablish, strengthen, settle you"* (1 Peter 5:10).

After you have suffered a little while, God will make you perfect and lead you into a place of settlement. After the pain, you are not left alone or disregarded. God will take you and perfect His will in your life.

The pain you experience will be your story, written by God and needs to be shared with others. This scripture proves that God knows we will have to endure certain circumstances that may be bitter. He knows that things will happen that will hurt, but He promises to never leave you. The pain of your past will not last because you must fulfil your task. When you go through your situation, remain at the place where God will lead you. He will take you to your next phase.

**For Contemplation:**

1. Remember all things work together for good to them that love God. Job's situation did not last, and yours won't either.

**NOTES:**

________________________________________

________________________________________

________________________________________

**Prayer changes things and people; make it a priority.**

# Day 246

*"God will look for someone who will teach their generation to fear Him."*

*"Seeing that Abraham shall surely become a great and mighty nation, and all the nations of the earth shall be blessed in him? For I know him, that he will command his children and his household after him, and they shall keep the way of the Lord, to do justice and judgment; that the Lord may bring upon Abraham that which he hath spoken of him"* (Genesis 18:18-19).

Many can say they know God, but it is a greater privilege when God says He knows you. God chose Abraham because He could trust Him to carry on His principles.

We have to ensure that God can trust our hearts with His standards and precepts. He needs to know that you are in His control. He needs to know that you love Him sincerely and you will keep His word so that you will not do anything that displeases Him. Sometimes, you do things that will displease God, but He will look to see if you will see yourself and turn from your own ways. Cause yourself to be in the sight of God, do things that attract the eyes of God to you. Do things that honour God, He will look out for you.

**For Contemplation:**

1. How does God see you? Do you know His standards and precepts? Can He trust your heart with them?

**NOTES:**

________________________________________

________________________________________

________________________________________

**Prayer changes things and people; make it a priority.**

# Day 247

---

***"You have already conquered every battle through the Victorious One."***

---

*"Nay, in all these things we are more than conquerors through Him that loved us"*( Romans 8:37) .

You are already more than a conqueror even before facing the battle. You are a champion through Christ Jesus. The moment Christ rose from the dead, we were immediately transformed into conquerors. He was given all power, and He gave some of this power to us.

The power that we have through the Spirit of God now anoints us with a champion anointing. Things that we were not able to do before we had the presence of God, we are now able to do. It does not matter the extent of the situation, you have conquered it. It is our responsibility to live our lives with the mentality of a champion.

**For Contemplation:**

1. Who is a conqueror? Whatever your definition, remember you are more than that through Christ Jesus.

**NOTES:**

___

___

___

**Prayer changes things and people; make it a priority.**

# Day 248

***"Learn how to put everything down to focus on the One you love."***

*"O God, thou art my God; early will I seek thee: my soul thirsteth for thee, my flesh longeth for thee in a dry and thirsty land, where no water is"* (Psalm 63:1 ).

The cares of the world will distract you from seeking God. You have to learn how to ignore the distraction and focus on who you say you love. In the natural, when a person 'loves' someone, people often say they are blinded by love. Meaning they are living a life dedicated to the person they love so much that their days are consumed by them.

Before you start the day, try to spend time with God. Make it your point of duty to seek Jesus and love Him. Show God that He is your priority, not your advances in life.

**For Contemplation:**

1. How often do you give God your undivided attention? Make God your priority in all areas of your life.

**NOTES:**

________________________________________

________________________________________

________________________________________

**Prayer changes things and people; make it a priority.**

# Day 249

***You are licensed to be violent in the spirit."***

*"And from the days of John the Baptist until now, the kingdom of heaven suffereth violence, and the violent take it by force"* (Matthew 11:12).

If you are walking in the Spirit of God, then you are licensed to be violent. This violence is not portrayed in the physical realm, but only applicable to the spiritual realm.

God has given you the legal right to be violent in the spirit. You are violent in order to take things by force. It is not to hurt anyone, but it is given to you to grab hold of something that heaven has released for you. You cannot be complacent when it comes to the things of the Spirit. The spirit realm moves very fast and if you are not sensitive you can miss seasons and opportunities.

Learn to be sensitive to the move of the spirit, this will allow you to do prophetic actions that will seal the things in the spirit to make them permanent. When they are made permanent, then they will manifest physically.

**For Contemplation:**

1. Have you been using your legal right to be violent in the spirit?

**NOTES:**

______________________________________________

______________________________________________

______________________________________________

**Prayer changes things and people; make it a priority.**

# Day 250

***"It is knowledge of the truth of God that causes freedom."***

*"And ye shall know the truth, and the truth shall make you free"* (John 8:32 ).

You can only know the truth by continuing in the Word of God, which is the book of truth. If you want the truth, study the Word of God. As you know the truth, you will now live your life according to the truth of God. Knowing the truth of God causes you to stand fast even in the midst of other false theories and doctrines. As people come with their many beliefs and opinions, you need to know that your opinion does not have the final word. It is the Word of God.

Freedom comes from knowledge of the truth. There is power in truth. Truth dispels all uncertainty. As you continue in the word of God, and know the truth you are now able to live life without uncertainty. You are sure of who you are and to Whom you belong. You will live knowing that your life is secured in the hands of God and that all things will work together for your good.

**For Contemplation:**

1. The only way to know the truth is to spend time in the Word, pray for revelation, and ask God for understanding.

**NOTES:**

______________________________________________

______________________________________________

______________________________________________

**Prayer changes things and people; make it a priority.**

# Day 251

***"Failure is not failure, unless you fail to try again."***

*"For a just man falleth seven times, and riseth up again: but the wicked shall fall into mischief"* (Proverbs 24:16).

Actual failure only comes when you choose to stay in that place of failure. If you choose not to try again, then you have failed. But even if you fail time after time, when you try again, your failures turn into lessons. This allows you to know what to do differently the next time you try again.

Failure does not define you; it can lead to success. When you fall down, get up and try again. Failure is not the end state for you as a child of God; you have an expected end, and you are not expected to fail.

**For Contemplation:**

1. Whether it be business, a hobby, school, or life in general, never stop with a failure. Seek the wisdom of God, make notes of the lessons you learned, find scriptures to support them, and be sure to try again.

NOTES:

---

---

---

**Prayer changes things and people; make it a priority.**

# Day 252

---

***"The weakest Christian in church is more powerful than any witch or wizard."***

---

*" But as many as received Him, to them gave he power to become the sons of God, even to them that believe on His name"* (John 1:12).

As long as you are a child of God, you are more powerful than the agents of the devil. You should not be afraid of them. Even if you have just been baptized, you are held in the hand of God. The devil cannot touch you.

Sons of God refer to angels, but as you receive Jesus in your heart, you become a son of God. You are higher than the fallen angels and the agents of the devil. When you are in God, there is a hedge around you. This hedge gives you an edge in life. Only if you break this hedge then the serpent has the opportunity to bite you. Keep yourself grounded in God and He will sustain you.

**For Contemplation:**

1. Once you belong to the Kingdom of Heaven, you are greater than any force of evil because of God. You need to spend time learning and understanding how great you are and unlocking your powers in God.

NOTES:

---

---

---

**Prayer changes things and people; make it a priority.**

# Day 253

---

***"Anger disarms the angered."***

---

*"When a strong man armed keepeth his palace, his goods are in peace: But when a stronger than he shall come upon him, and overcome him, he taketh from him all his armour wherein he trusted, and divideth his spoils"* (Luke 11:21-22) .

When an angered man is disarmed, then he is opened to the adversary to affect him. If a stronger man comes to this man, then the strong man is able to spoil him. If a man becomes angry, then his mind is clouded, and this may blind him from seeing someone who comes to rob them. This can happen to Christians; if you remove yourself from the hedge that God placed around you because of external forces, then things can affect you. Ensure that you do not become disarmed.

**For Contemplation:**

1. How do you deal with situations when you are angry? Remember temperance is a fruit of the spirit.

NOTES:

---

---

---

**Prayer changes things and people; make it a priority.**

# Day 254

***" You have a choice to react negatively or positively to your problems."***

*"As sorrowful, yet always rejoicing; as poor, yet making many rich; as having nothing, and yet possessing all things"* (2 Corinthians 6:10).

It is your choice to cry or rejoice during your troubles. You have the choice to be happy in the face of adversity or allow it to dull your emotions. You are expected to rejoice in the Lord, always. You can choose to react to your reality or react based on the reality you have in God. The reality of the world will pass away, but the reality of God lasts forever. Stand in the infiniteness of God rather than in the temporary nature of the world.

**For Contemplation:**

1. Recall the last time you heard bad news, what was it and how did you react? Was it the reaction of a conqueror? Be conscious and intentional, choose to stand on the Word of God above all else.

**NOTES:**

______________________________________________

______________________________________________

______________________________________________

**Prayer changes things and people; make it a priority.**

# Day 255

***" You cannot fight what you are afraid of."***

*"The fear of man bringeth a snare: but whoso putteth his trust in the Lord shall be safe"*( Proverbs 29:25).

If you are fearful of something. It means you have been defeated by that thing in your mind already. Being defeated in the mind causes you to be defeated before you even face your fears.

When you fear something, it has more power over you and presents itself before you. The more your mind thinks about it, the more physical it will become. You have to overcome this fear by trusting in God's love. Love is God. When you trust in God, you have everything you need to overcome your fears, being confident that love protects.

**For Contemplation:**

1. Fear will cripple you and cause you to run from your shadow. Whenever you are afraid, encourage yourself in the Lord. Remember there is power in you and there's no place for fear.

**NOTES:**

______________________________________________

______________________________________________

______________________________________________

**Prayer changes things and people; make it a priority.**

# Day 256

***" If you do not understand the value of something, you won't go out of your way to get it."***

*"Again, the kingdom of heaven is like unto a merchant, seeking goodly pearls: Who, when he had found one pearl of great price, went and sold all that he had, and bought it"* (Matthew 13:45-46).

The way you treat something indicates how much you value it. When you value something others will see it clearly. When you value something you will make extraordinary sacrifices to get it, and you will go through great lengths to maintain it.

The kingdom of heaven is likened unto an invaluable

pearl. It was so valuable that the man sold all that he had to obtain this unique pearl. What sacrifices have you made to be in the kingdom of God? The man knew that the value of the pearl would cost all that he had. He had many things, but he sold all that he had to get one precious pearl. It could be that he may never find a pearl like this again, and so he took the opportunity without looking at the extent of his sacrifice. He didn't want to pass up this 'once in a lifetime' opportunity. Persons may have discouraged him and called him crazy, and asked him why he would give up all for just one thing. As we freely received salvation, we had to make sacrifices that may not have been to the extent of this man's sacrifice to keep our salvation, but we had to make certain decisions that denied our flesh from being satisfied.

We have to recognize that we have the most valuable gift, we have the gift of salvation. We did not have to be saved by God, but He chose to save us, and now we are joint heirs with Jesus because of His unconditional love toward us. Jesus is the best gift. Many say when a baby is born, it is the gift of life. But life does not start until you are born again. Born again means you are now born of the Spirit of God. You are now in His Kingdom; the King of all kings is now your Father. We have hope in God, He has our lives in His hands.

**For Contemplation:**

1. Spend three minutes to thank God for giving you something that cannot be bought or sold in stores. Work out your salvation each day with fear and trembling.

**NOTES:**

________________________________________

________________________________________

________________________________________

**Prayer changes things and people; make it a priority.**

# Day 257

***"You cannot continue to dream from another person's. You must be careful of the decisions that you make, as you can be influenced by a spirit."***

*"And the Lord said, Who shall persuade Ahab, that he may go up and fall at Ramoth Gilead? And one said on this manner, and another said on that manner. And there came forth a spirit, and stood before the Lord, and said, I will persuade him. And the Lord said unto him, Wherewith? And he said, I will go forth, and I will be a lying spirit in the mouth of all his prophets. And he said, Thou shalt persuade him, and prevail also: go forth, and do so"* (1 Kings 22:20-22).

In this scripture we see that spirits can influence the thoughts and actions of man. The king of Israel, Ahab wanted to know if he should go into Ramothgilead to fight. Then the king of Judah, Jehoshaphat told Ahab that he should ask for God's instructions. All the prophets in the land were gathered before the kings and they were asked what God said about the matter, and all said that King Ahab would be victorious. King Jehoshaphat found this very suspicious, and he asked, isn't there anyone else who will say something different. King Ahab said there was one more prophet, Micaiah, but he has always prophesied evil.

When Micaiah stood before the kings, he spoke the same as the previous prophets. King Ahab asked Micaiah to tell him the truth. Micaiah began to tell him what he saw in heaven, as God was asking who would persuade Ahab to go to Ramoth Gilead. The Bible says a spirit appeared before the Lord and said it will go and be a lying spirit in the prophets, that they will prophesy good things that the king wants to hear. A spirit caused the prophets to lie.

Always be careful when making a decision, and whatever the decision is ask yourself if there was a motive. If there is a motive then it becomes easy for a spirit to influence you, causing you to shift more to the side of the motive. Ensure that anything you do, there is no possibility of another spirit's influence other than God's spirit.

**For Contemplation:**

1. How do you make decisions? Do you seek counsel from a leader, coworker, or friend? Are your decisions supported by scripture?

**NOTES:**

________________________________________

________________________________________

________________________________________

**Prayer changes things and people; make it a priority.**

# Day 258

***"The Spirit of God inside of you has the ability to know everything."***

*"But God hath revealed them unto us by His Spirit: for the Spirit searcheth all things, yea, the deep things of God. For what man knoweth the things of a man, save the spirit of man which is in him? Even so the things of God knoweth no man, but the Spirit of God"* (1 Corinthians 2:10-11) .

The Spirit of God within us searches out all things, therefore knowing all things. God is all-knowing, hence as His children, His Spirit operates within us. Our spirit was built for the Spirit of God, as only spirit can sync spirit. The more we sync our spirits with God's Spirit, the more we access the God-potential within us.

There is no limit to what the Spirit of God in us can do. As you remember all the miracles that Jesus did here on earth, remember also, that He said that greater will we do. We should be confident in the God who lives in us. *"But the Comforter, which is the Holy Ghost, whom the Father will send in my name, He shall teach you all things, and bring all things to your remembrance, whatsoever I have said unto you"* (John 14:26).

The Holy Spirit will teach you all things, hence you can know all things. The Spirit within you can know things even before they happen and so when you are led by the Spirit then your actions will align with what the Spirit of God knows.

**For Contemplation:**

1. Do you rely on the Holy Spirit which is inside of you? How often do you consult with the Holy Spirit?

**NOTES:**

______________________________________________

______________________________________________

______________________________________________

**Prayer changes things and people; make it a priority.**

# Day 259

***"You cannot force God's hands through prayer."***

*"For this thing, I besought the Lord thrice, that it might depart from me. And He said unto me, My grace is sufficient for thee: for my strength is made perfect in weakness. Most gladly, therefore, will I rather glory in my infirmities, that the power of Christ may rest upon me"* (2 Corinthians 12:8-9) .

There are times when we repeatedly ask God for something, because we haven't seen it yet. If we consistently go to God with a request after we say we believe that we have received, it can signify lack of faith in God. However, the Bible also speaks on persistent praying, which shows our dependence on God. These two opinions are valid; however, we must go deeper and analyze them.

In the scripture above, Paul went to God about a matter three times. Even though Paul wanted to be free from this situation, God already gave him the answer, no. God wanted to use the situation Paul was going through to show that His power can be manifested even in our times of suffering. Sometimes, the challenges we go through are testing periods that build our faith in God, but most of us want to be free from our challenges immediately, and some may not even want to go through any difficulty. However, these situations humble us before God, and allow His true strength to be seen in our weaknesses. After Paul understood what God was trying to say, he desisted from praying about the matter and simply trusted in God.

The Bible also tells us that men should always pray (Luke 18:1). While we are always expected to pray, there are times when God has already released our answers, and we should receive it by faith. It doesn't mean that you should stop praying, but remember the primary reason for prayer is to communicate with God. It is not to force Him to do something on our behalf. You should not try to use prayer as a weapon to try to manipulate the hand of God. There is nothing wrong with desiring good gifts from God, but it should never be your priority; God is. Praying repeatedly should not be done like it is a magic trick; the more you pray, the faster it will come. Instead, when you pray and let your request be made known to Him, you will receive your answer and begin thanking Him for what He has promised you; remind Him of His word. Do not treat prayer unto God, as a spoiled child always asking his parent for something, after the parent has already said no or told them to wait. You can't force God's hands, He is not obligated to us. He is the promise-keeping God, and if He says something, He will do it.

**For Contemplation:**

1. Read John 9. The man was blind that the works of God should be made manifest in him. Some situations you are faced with is for God to get His glory. What is God saying about your situation?

NOTES:

---

---

---

**Prayer changes things and people; make it a priority.**

# Day 260

---

***" The church is the intercessor for a nation."***

---

*"And He taught, saying unto them, Is it not written, My house shall be called of all nations the house of prayer? but ye have made it a den of thieves"* (Mark 11:17 ).

Jesus was not pleased with the way the people dishonoured the holy temple. He overthrew tables of persons who were selling and chased them out, after which He said, *"My house shall be called of all nations a house of prayer"*.

The church is the voice of God to the nations. Therefore, we must be in constant prayer in order to hear the voice of God. The church should prioritize prayer. This means deliberately setting aside specific times dedicated to prayer. There is tremendous power when the church prays. As we corporately pray, the power is released because there is agreement in Jesus' Name.

*"I exhort therefore, that, first of all, supplications, prayers, intercessions, and giving of thanks, be made for all men; For kings, and for all that are in authority; that we may lead a quiet and peaceable life in all godliness and honesty"* (1 Timothy 2:1-2).

The church should make intercession for all men. It should be the intercessor for men on earth to the Father in heaven. We are instructed to pray for the leaders of our country and those in positions of authority so that we will live peacefully in our country.

**For Contemplation:**

1. Participate in the corporate fasting and prayers your church calls. It is our duty and responsibility to intercede for the nation.

**NOTES:**

______________________________________________

______________________________________________

______________________________________________

**Prayer changes things and people; make it a priority.**

# Day 261

***" Never condemn yourself when you do something wrong."***

*"There is therefore now no condemnation to them which are in Christ Jesus, who walk not after the flesh, but after the Spirit"(* Romans 8:1).

Condemn means to disapprove or sentence someone to a punishment. You do not have to condemn yourself when you do something wrong. It is natural to feel disappointed in yourself when you do, but you should never condemn.

We were all born sinners, but it was even in our sinful state that Christ came and died for us so that we would not be condemned to hell or eternal torment. *"If we say that we have no sin, we deceive ourselves, and the truth is not in us. If we confess our sins, He is faithful and just to forgive us our sins, and to cleanse us from all unrighteousness"* (1 John 1:8-9).

We should never remove ourselves from the presence of God when we sin. Sin will cause you to hide yourself. It makes you feel ashamed, and this causes many people to stop going to church, praying, and having a relationship with God. The fact that you feel guilty about what you have done, indicates that you still have a love for God, which can change your situation immensely.

Remember the grace of God covers a multitude of sin. Your sins are not bigger than God, and neither are you.

**For Contemplation:**

1. Forgive yourself for your sins and transgressions. Learn from your mistakes, apply what you learn, and keep growing.

**NOTES:**

---

---

---

**Prayer changes things and people; make it a priority.**

# Day 262

---

*"Many Christians are living at the 'outer court' dimension."*

---

*"And when they go forth into the outer court, even into the outer court to the people, they shall put off their garments wherein they ministered, and lay them in the holy chambers, and they shall put on other garments; and they shall not sanctify the people with their garments"* (Ezekiel 44:19).

If you live in the flesh, you live in the 'outer court' dimension. The outer court of the temple of God was the place where sins were dealt with. They were not dealt with in the inner courts, as this was the place of holiness, and sin could not enter there. The brazen altar and the brazen laver were present in the outer courts. On the altar the animal was killed and blood was shed. The flesh dies at the altar. The brazen laver was used for washing, representing the washing of your sins and transformation from unholy to holy. This is synonymous with water baptism. The outer court represent where you are being introduced to God, for example, during an altar call.

After the priest does the sacrifice and symbolic washing, then he is now permitted to go into the temple and beyond the veil. However, some Christians are still stuck in the outer court where they are introduced to Jesus, they accept Him, but they do not have encounters with Him. The verse highlighted said that when the priest was returning from within the temple, he had to remove his clothes before returning to the outer court where the children of Israel were. The very clothes that were worn in the presence of God could sanctify the people, and this was why the priest had to remove them before returning to the crowd. The clothes were holy. Holiness is to become one with God, and this can only happen when you go beyond the outer court.

It is time for us all to become one with God, it is time to have encounters with Him in the inner court. There is too much distraction in the outer court.

**For Contemplations**

1. Stay far from sin, live holy for holiness is to become one with God.

**NOTES:**

______________________________________________

______________________________________________

______________________________________________

**Prayer changes things and people; make it a priority.**

# Day 263

***" The content within a container makes the price of the product expensive."***

*"Ye are of God, little children, and have overcome them: because greater is He that is in you than He that is in the world"* (1 John 4:4).

If the container does not dictate the price, it is the content that carries the value. When you go to the supermarket or store, the container attracts you based on its beauty. However, the content is the determining factor for your purchase. Sometimes, the container can be attractive, but the content is not good.

We are the children of God, and we have Him on our inside. Hence, because we have the Spirit of God on our inside, we are greater than anyone in the world who does not have Him on their inside. This means we should not be afraid. We have the greater One inside of us, and He is the King of kings. We carry His glory, so wherever we go, we can change the atmosphere.

**For Contemplation:**

1. What is on your inside? What are the desires of your heart?

**NOTES:**

________________________________________

________________________________________

________________________________________

**Prayer changes things and people; make it a priority.**

# Day 264

***" The Spirit of God is light. If a man walks by His Spirit, his light shines brighter."***

*"Let your light so shine before men, that they may see your good works, and glorify your Father which is in heaven."* Matthew 5:16).

The light of God should easily radiate from you. As you continue to walk by the Spirit of God, the more His light should shine through you. This light serves as a signal that attracts other people to you so that they can get saved as well and come to serve God.

As God's light shines, it also clearly shows you where you are going. God is leading you. This light can benefit others on their journey and help them see as well. Continue to allow the light of God to shine through as you lead others to Him.

**For Contemplation:**

1. Encourage a believer in your workplace that is surrounded by unbelievers to continue shining bright for others to see and glorify God.

**NOTES:**

______________________________________________

______________________________________________

______________________________________________

**Prayer changes things and people; make it a priority.**

# Day 265

*"The Word of God satisfies you."*

*"But he answered and said, It is written, Man shall not live by bread alone, but by every word that proceedeth out of the mouth of God" (Matthew 4:4 ).*

The word of God satisfies us, rather than physical food. We have been grown in such a way that makes us believe that we cannot survive without physical food. However, the scripture states that we should not live by bread alone. This is not the main source of our survival as children of God, it is the Word of God.

The Word of God is the food which our spirits need to survive in the world. Our spirits can only prosper if we are feeding it with the things of God. The Word of God can bring restoration.

**For Contemplation:**

1. How often do you feed your spirit? Remember, natural bread alone won't keep you.

NOTES:

______________________________________________

______________________________________________

______________________________________________

**Prayer changes things and people; make it a priority.**

# Day 266

***Faith is always outside the realm of your senses."***

*"For we walk by faith, not by sight"* (2 Corinthians 5: 7).

Faith is coupled with appropriate actions. These actions are not based on our emotions or what we see or feel. The issues that we see, hear, and feel can impact our faith in God and decrease it. Do not allow situations external to God to affect your faith in God.

When giving by faith, you have to remove yourself from your senses, and zoom into what you want, meditate on it and then give. Do not give out of your emotions or by pressure. Give as you are led by the Spirit. A man of faith who believes and knows, speaks to see. A man of flesh, sees to speak.

**For Contemplation:**

1. Faith comes by hearing. If you find yourself lacking faith, listen to the testimonies of others, read the stories of the Bible, and remind yourself that God is able.

NOTES:

______________________________________________

______________________________________________

______________________________________________

**Prayer changes things and people; make it a priority.**

# Day 267

*" Yoke yourself with Jesus."*

*"Come unto me, all ye that labour and are heavy laden, and I will give you rest. Take my yoke upon you, and learn of me; for I am meek and lowly in heart: and ye shall find rest unto your souls. For my yoke is easy, and my burden is light"* (Matthew 11:28-30).

We can only find true rest in Jesus. You cannot use your soul or mind to rest, you need the peace of Jesus. You can have His peace even in the midst of chaos.

A yoke is a wooden device that is fastened around the neck of two animals connecting them. Jesus wants us to Take His yoke because it is easy. We can yoke ourselves to Jesus so that wherever He goes, we have no choice but to move with Him. Remember, we are joint heirs with Him; therefore, His inheritance also becomes our inheritance. His ways become our ways until they are permanently within us. His burden, unlike ours, is light. Yoke yourself with Jesus; He wants to give you rest.

**For Contemplation:**

1. Take Jesus' yoke upon you and learn of Him. Who is Jesus to you? What does he require of you? What are His characteristics?

**NOTES:**

________________________________________________

________________________________________________

________________________________________________

**Prayer changes things and people; make it a priority.**

# Day 268

*" Light attracts light, but it also attracts unwanted things. "*

*"Arise, shine; for thy light is come, and the glory of the Lord is risen upon thee. For, behold, the darkness shall cover the earth, and gross darkness the people: but the Lord shall arise upon thee, and His glory shall be seen upon thee. And the Gentiles shall come to thy light, and kings to the brightness of thy rising"* ( Isaiah 60:1-3).

Have you ever seen insects attracted to light, especially when there is only one light source in the midst of darkness? You will see these insects swarming around the light. Light serves many purposes, and every living thing responds to light.

As your light can attract others who have light, you will also attract evil to you. As verse 3 says, Gentiles will come to our light. Gentiles meant people who were not Jews, they are not the people of God. But if they come to the light and accept the gift of salvation then they will be transformed by the light into light.

**For Contemplation:**

1. Wherever you go, let your light so shine before men, that they may see your good works and glorify your Father, who is in heaven.

**NOTES:**

____________________________________________________

____________________________________________________

____________________________________________________

**Prayer changes things and people; make it a priority.**

# Day 269

***" It takes a champion, to kill a champion."***

*"And as he talked with them, behold, there came up the champion, the Philistine of Gath, Goliath by name, out of the armies of the Philistines, and spake according to the same words: and David heard them. And all the men of Israel, when they saw the man, fled from him, and were sore*

*afraid. And David put his hand in his bag, and took thence a stone, and slang it, and smote the Philistine in his forehead, that the stone sunk into his forehead; and he fell upon his face to the earth. So David prevailed over the Philistine with a sling and with a stone, and smote the Philistine, and slew him; but there was no sword in the hand of David. Therefore David ran, and stood upon the Philistine, and took his sword, and drew it out of the sheath thereof, and slew him, and cut off his head therewith. And when the Philistines saw their champion was dead, they fled.*
(1 Samuel 17:23-24, 49-51) .

As we know the story of David and Goliath, we must recognize that God has champions, but the devil also has his champions. It takes a champion to recognize a champion, and it takes one to defeat one. If you are a champion, you know your team's strengths, as well as their weaknesses. Champions are born out of difficulty. An anointing rests upon those who are champions in God. Like how David was anointed by the prophet of God. This anointing will carry you through difficult times. The anointing from God will interact with something that is inside of you.

When a champion is defeated the people who followed him will flee, when they see that their champion is dead.

**For Contemplation:**

1. What is your Goliath? How can you become David?

**NOTES:**

________________________________________

________________________________________

________________________________________

**Prayer changes things and people; make it a priority.**

# Day 270

***"Many champions are overlooked because of how they look."***

*"But the Lord said unto Samuel, Look not on his countenance, or on the height of his stature; because I have refused him: for the Lord seeth not as man seeth; for man looketh on the outward appearance, but the Lord looketh on the heart… Again, Jesse made seven of his sons to pass before Samuel. And Samuel said unto Jesse, The Lord hath not chosen these. And Samuel said unto Jesse, Are here all thy children? And he said, There remaineth yet the youngest, and, behold, he keepeth the sheep. And Samuel said unto Jesse, Send and fetch him: for we will not sit down till he come hither. And he sent, and brought him in. Now he was ruddy, and withal of a beautiful countenance, and goodly to look to. And the Lord said, Arise, anoint him: for this is he"* (1 Samuel 16:7, 10-12) .

David was overlooked because of his stature, but he was the one who killed the giant. Sometimes, champions can be overlooked because of their appearance. Their appearance doesn't meet people's expectations of how a champion is supposed to look. People look at appearance, but God looks at the heart. He will never make the mistake that Samuel made.

Do not worry about how you look, or where you are right now. God's disguise will confound the wise. God is the one that qualifies man, He is the one who chooses who He wants to use. He is the One that will cause the oil to flow for you. Your champion may not manifest immediately, but it will at the ideal time.

**For Contemplation:**

1. Be concerned about how you look in the spiritual not in the natural.

NOTES:

---

**Prayer changes things and people; make it a priority.**

# Day 271

***" Life is not how you feel to live it, you have a destiny."***

*'For I know the thoughts that I think toward you, saith the Lord, thoughts of peace, and not of evil, to give you an expected end"*( Jeremiah 29:11).

You cannot live your life anyhow you want and any way you please. Your life is for a specific reason. You have a destiny from God to fulfill here on earth. Your life is not for yourself, but you are living for someone, your family, and a generation.

**For Contemplation:**

1. Your choices can affect your life. Be sure to consult with God before making all decisions. Always aim to be in alignment with your purpose; your destiny helper may be searching for you.

NOTES:

---

**Prayer changes things and people; make it a priority.**

# Day 272

***" God looked like He was sending Joseph into harm's way, but he was in God's arms."***

*field: and the man asked him, saying, What seekest thou? And he said, I seek my brethren: tell me, I pray thee, where they feed their flocks. And the man said, They are departed hence; for I heard them say, Let us go to Dothan. And Joseph went after his brethren, and found them in Dothan. And when they saw him afar off, even before he came near unto them, they conspired against him to slay him"* (Genesis 37:15-18).

It appeared as if Joseph was set in harm's way. However, all these were steps towards his true destiny. It may look so in our lives, as we see the different situations we face. Others may be wondering why we may go through certain things and we are children of God, and then this may cause us to start wondering.

Even though life may seem challenging, we should remain at peace, knowing that we have God with us. God has plans for you and it may not seem like a secure way, but God knows your destiny.

**For Contemplation:**

1. The Angel of the Lord told Mary she was highly favored, yet she was ridiculed for being unmarried and pregnant. You may frustrate yourself trying to figure out God's plans. Trust God's Word, trust the process, trust God.

**NOTES:**

________________________________________

________________________________________

________________________________________

**Prayer changes things and people; make it a priority.**

# Day 273

***" When you encounter God, your life must change."***

*"A new heart also will I give you, and a new spirit will I put within you: and I will take away the stony heart out of your flesh, and I will give you*

*an heart of flesh. And I will put my spirit within you, and cause you to walk in my statutes, and ye shall keep my judgments, and do them"* (Ezekiel 36:26-27) .

You have to see change after you meet God. The Lord will give you a different heart, one that is more receptive of His Word and ways. He will give you a heart that will yearn more for the things of God.

**For Contemplation:**

1. How has your life changed since encountering God? Write down at least 2 examples.

**NOTES:**

---

**Prayer changes things and people; make it a priority.**

# Day 274

---

***" A receiver has an attitude, position and a signal."***

---

*"Now Hannah, she spake in her heart; only her lips moved, but her voice was not heard: therefore Eli thought she had been drunken. And Eli said unto her, How long wilt thou be drunken? put away thy wine from thee. And Hannah answered and said, No, my lord, I am a woman of a sorrowful spirit: I have drunk neither wine nor strong drink, but have poured out my soul before the Lord. Count not thine handmaid for a daughter of Belial: for out of the abundance of my complaint and grief have I spoken hitherto. Then Eli answered and said, Go in peace: and the God of Israel grant thee thy petition that thou hast asked of him. And she said, Let thine handmaid find grace in thy sight. So the woman went her way, and did eat, and her countenance was no more sad"* (1 Samuel 1:13 -18).

We will examine the story of Hannah who was barren and was not able to get pregnant. We see that Hannah wants to receive this gift from the Lord. She was very sad about the situation that she was in, and so she was seen praying to God. At first, Eli thought she was drunk because he heard no words coming from her, but rather, she spoke in her heart to God.

After Eli told her that she should go in peace, Hannah's countenance changed, and she was not sad anymore. Hannah's attitude changed. The attitude of the receiver shows where their heart is to receive. This affects position, and position influences the signal that is given off.

Hannah was in a place of bitterness, but her attitude changed, she was not sad any more. This could be seen in the signals that she gave off. Hannah went from a place of fasting to feasting. She did not wait until she physically received it, once her spirit received it everything changed. After receiving prophetic words, what have you done? She found peace in the words from Eli; she believed that God would come through for her, and indeed, the Lord did. You have to learn to contend for your prophecy. Declare them and remind God of His word.

**For Contemplation:**

1. Assess your posture for receiving miracles and breakthroughs.

**NOTES:**

______________________________________________

______________________________________________

______________________________________________

**Prayer changes things and people; make it a priority.**

# Day 275

---

*" When you pray, God bottles and stores your prayers."*

---

*"And when he had taken the book, the four beasts and four and twenty elders fell down before the Lamb, having every one of them harps, and golden vials full of odours, which are the prayers of saints"* (Revelation 5:8).

Your prayers are valuable to God. When you pray sincerely to God, you must understand that He collects all and stores them. The Lord takes joy when His people come to Him in prayer. This is how we communicate with Him.

**For Contemplation:**

1. Use this week to increase your prayer bank, pray for men in authority, the nation, your family, and yourself.

**NOTES:**

______________________________________________

______________________________________________

______________________________________________

**Prayer changes things and people; make it a priority.**

# Day 276

***" Joy is in your spirit, but others can see and sense your joy."***

*"These things have I spoken unto you, that my joy might remain in you, and that your joy might be full"*( John 15:11).

Others around you can see the effects of joy in you. Just as Jesus granted us Joy, we can also help others to experience joy. Our outward countenance displays what we have on our insides. If we are joyful, this can be seen. The same applies to us when we are sad.

**For Contemplation:**

1. Help someone today to experience joy. Whether it is by blessing them, smiling, offering a favour or simply doing a tedious task for them. Spread some joy today.

**NOTES:**

---

---

---

**Prayer changes things and people; make it a priority.**

# Day 277

***" When you minister to someone, you have to minister to the mind."***

*"For as he thinketh in his heart, so is he: Eat and drink, saith he to thee; but his heart is not with thee"* (Proverbs 23:7).

The mind is a powerful tool that all humans have. Many thoughts and ideas are formulated here. You cannot affect a person unless you get to the mind. You have to ensure that you connect to the mind of the person because as you speak, the mind is working and coming up with different reasons why they should or should not listen to you. The mindset has to change in order for there to be a change. As you change the thoughts of someone, then they will think of themselves in that way. A person may have faith on the inside, but it will be difficult for them to believe if their mind is not there.

**For Contemplation:**

1. Pray to God about the person you're planning to introduce to God. Ask the Holy Spirit to guide you as you minister to people. Remember, different fish require a different hook to be

caught. A shark cannot be caught with the same hook as a sprat.

**NOTES:**

---

---

---

**Prayer changes things and people; make it a priority.**

# Day 278

---

***" Let your words be like money, spend them wisely."***

---

*"Let no corrupt communication proceed out of your mouth, but that which is good to the use of edifying, that it may minister grace unto the hearer" (*Ephesians 4:29 ).

Your words are an important currency here on earth. If you do not use them well, then you will not profit from them. The words that we speak should not cause negative situations to manifest in our lives, as words are supposed to bring forth and encourage life, not death.

We have to speak the right words, at the right time in the right place. Corrupt or foul speech should not be in the mouths of children of God. This dishonours God and creates a certain atmosphere around us that can be destructive or undesirable. When we speak, we are instructed to edify. This means our words should not tear down anyone, instead we should build them up. The words we speak should improve a person's state and not ruin it. If we need to correct someone, we must still do so in love.

Your words should not kill, but create.

**For Contemplation:**

1. Be mindful of the words you speak over your life and the lives of those around you.

NOTES:

---

---

---

**Prayer changes things and people; make it a priority.**

# Day 279

***" You have the light and glory of God within you, all you need to do is release a sound."***

*"And God said, Let there be light: and there was light"* (Genesis 1:3).

In Genesis 3, God had three things when He was creating. He had His glory, He had light and He had a sound. God spoke, "Let there be light", and immediately there was light. God then continued speaking things into being, in the presence of light and His glory.

He is the Creator, and no one can compare to Him because He made something out of nothing. He only used His words. Inventors and scientists on earth need something that already exists to create something new. This is not so with God. He spoke into nothingness. He had no help, no building material. He spoke.

Therefore, as His children, we have the light and the glory of God within us; all we need to do is to release a sound. The sound has vibrations that cause a shift, which affects the glory and light and shapes it into what you desire to see. We need to understand that we have this authority through Jesus Christ.

**For Contemplation:**

1. List the 7 miracles Elijah performed. Because of Christ Jesus we are greater than Elijah, speak your breakthrough into being.

NOTES:

---

---

---

**Prayer changes things and people; make it a priority.**

# Day 280

***" If you are not anointed to handle the presence of God, do not touch it."***

*"And he smote the men of Bethshemesh, because they had looked into the ark of the Lord, even he smote of the people fifty thousand and threescore and ten men: and the people lamented, because the Lord had smitten many of the people with a great slaughter"* (1 Samuel 6:19).

When we become familiar with the presence of God, there can be consequences. In this scripture, we see that God killed many people because they looked into the ark of the covenant. The ark represented His holy presence in the midst of the Israelites. This passage encourages us to ensure that we follow the precepts of God when it comes to honouring His presence. We may believe that the ways we honour Him are right, however, if they are not according to God's standards, we will face consequences.

We can also examine the same sixth chapter of 2 Samuel. *"And when they came to Nachon's threshing floor, Uzzah put forth his hand to the ark of God, and took hold of it; for the oxen shook it. And the anger of the Lord was kindled against Uzzah; and God smote him there for his error; and there he died by the ark of God. And David was displeased, because the Lord had made a breach upon Uzzah: and he called the name of the place Perezuzzah to this day"* (2 Samuel 6:6-8 ).

Uzzah also had the same fate as the priests who desecrated the presence of God in 1 Samuel 6. However, he was genuinely trying to prevent the ark from falling to the ground. He was trying to save it because it was holy. However, God's anger was kindled and Uzzah died. David was upset with God because he knew Uzzah did it out of a good heart. But God was serious about His presence. Sometimes, we want to force ourselves to operate outside of God's grace in our lives. However, we shouldn't try to promote ourselves; rather, we do what God has called us to do now. He will promote you in due season. If you are not graced for something, do not do it from your own strength and flesh, you are not honouring God.

God's mercy may not always prevail in our errors; sometimes, His wrath will speak. We have to be very careful when we are in the presence of God. The actions we do in the presence of God should honour Him. We have to pray that we are constantly living according to God's standards and not our own or else we are deceiving ourselves. Sometimes, we may think that our actions are justified, but in God's eyes, it is an error. Ask God to teach you how He wants you to honour Him.

**For Contemplation:**

1. What is the ark of God and how should it be handled? Use scriptures to research this.

**NOTES:**

______________________________________________

______________________________________________

______________________________________________

**Prayer changes things and people; make it a priority.**

# Day 281

---

*" Jesus restored power to the fallen man."*

---

*"And when He had called unto Him His twelve disciples, He gave them power against unclean spirits, to cast them out, and to heal all manner of sickness and all manner of disease"* (Matthew 10:1).

Jesus restored mankind to their original place and authority in God. When Adam sinned, man lost their place in God. Instead of having dominion over the earth, man lost the benefits of being God's creation because of disobedience. Because of the fall of Adam, we have inherited the corruptible mind. We were born in sin and shaped in iniquity (Psalm 51:5).

But God gave us another chance of redemption. A way where we can retrieve our God-given rights. He sent His Son to die for us, even while we were still sinners. Adam fell in sin, but Christ fell to death so that He can remove our sins from us. When Christ fell, and died, as His blood was shed, we inherited the Blood of Jesus.

As we accept Jesus, we overcome the corruptible mind that we originally had and now we have the mind of Christ. We are saved and we are free from the law of sin. Therefore, we cannot be defeated by sin, sickness or the adversary. Jesus was our restorer of the breach between us and the Father.

**For Contemplation:**

1. What was God's judgement when Adam sinned?

**NOTES:**

________________________________________________

________________________________________________

________________________________________________

**Prayer changes things and people; make it a priority.**

# Day 282

***" As a seed of the righteous, begging is not your portion."***

*"I have been young, and now am old; yet have I not seen the righteous forsaken, nor his seed begging bread"*(Psalm 37:25).

You are not destined to suffer because of the plans of the enemy. You are the seed of the righteous, you are not sustained by begging. You are of the righteousness of God; therefore, the blessings that should follow a child of God must be seen in your life. The Lord will sustain you, He will never leave you nor forsake you. A good Father will never leave His children, and God will never leave you.

**For Contemplation:**

1. Remind someone today that God will never leave his children. Explain to them what this means.

**NOTES:**

________________________________________

________________________________________

________________________________________

**Prayer changes things and people; make it a priority.**

# Day 283

***" The strength of the walls determines the strength of a city."***

*"He shall not be afraid of evil tidings: his heart is fixed, trusting in the Lord."*( Psalm 112:7).

If you want to survive these times and the times to come upon this earth, your heart must be secured firmly in God. The deeper your heart is in God, the stronger your heart will be against the elements around you. As your heart is fixed within the foundations of God, you will not be afraid of anything. When you are not afraid, you will not shake. Therefore, your foundation in God is never compromised, it stands firm.

Your strength is anchored in God. From today you will walk in your prophetic overflow and manifestation. Your seed will not beg for bread.

**For Contemplation:**

1. How strong are your walls? How rooted are you in God?

**NOTES:**

______________________________________________

______________________________________________

______________________________________________

**Prayer changes things and people; make it a priority.**

# Day 284

***" Kadesh Barnea is your "look-out" spot, you have to be strategic in this area of your life."***

*"And Joshua the son of Nun sent out of Shittim two men to spy secretly, saying, Go view the land, even Jericho. And they went, and came into an harlot's house, named Rahab, and lodged there"* ( Joshua 2:1 ).

Kadesh means holy. Kadesh Barnea was a place where the Israelites mainly camped, before they entered their promised land. This is the place that prepares people to enter the full promises of God.

It is a place where you will have to trust God. This was the place where the Israelites lost battles. Your season in Kadesh Barnea may look as if the promises of God will never happen, but you must remain in God as your breakthrough is almost in sight.

This is the place where you are tested on patience and obedience.

As God is teaching you in this place, you must ensure that you learn and apply these lessons to your life accordingly. You have to learn to make strategic decisions. At this place, you can understand how the enemy operates, and in turn, you will know how to operate and be victorious.

For Contemplation:

1. Value your Kadesh Barnea. Learn the lessons being taught, make your strategic decisions, we are in a war. Stay focused.

**NOTES:**

---

---

---

**Prayer changes things and people; make it a priority.**

# Day 285

***"Death is the absence of the presence of God."***

*"And this is the record, that God hath given to us eternal life, and this life is in his Son. He that hath the Son hath life; and he that hath not the Son of God hath not life."* (1 John 5:11-12).

There are many walking-dead people around us, and it is our duty to introduce life to them. People in sin claim that they are living lives, because they have the latest cars, the finest clothes and money. However, if they do not have Jesus, they have not yet begun life.

Without God, there is no life. We need God to lead and direct us in the way we should live. His instructions are the blueprints for us. These steps must be followed precisely in order to see the potential of God within us on earth. Your life is hid in Christ (Colossian 3:3). Therefore, nothing can harm you as you are covered. As you are in Christ, you will have life and have it more abundantly.

**For Contemplation:**

1. Before closing the year, find a few dead people (sinners) and raise them up. Let them know life begins with Jesus.

**NOTES:**

____________________________________________

____________________________________________

____________________________________________

**Prayer changes things and people; make it a priority.**

# Day 286

***" Whatever area you live in, you need to search out what principality is controlling it."***

*"To the intent that now unto the principalities and powers in heavenly places might be known by the church the manifold wisdom of God"* (Ephesians 3:10).

Principalities rule over different territories. There are good and bad principalities and you must discern which is operating over the area in which reside or work.

You must be the spiritual watch over your neighbourhood. Witches and warlocks release curses over different areas, but the areas that are covered by the Blood of Jesus will be off-limits. As you watch the news and see how saddening it can be when we hear of the different events that happen in communities. We must know that these things are spiritual. Demons are released that seek life and blood and we must pray against these plans of the devil. We should never stop praying for our communities and our country.

**For Contemplation:**

1. What principality is in control over your community? Pray for your community against these principalities.

**NOTES:**

______________________________________________

______________________________________________

______________________________________________

**Prayer changes things and people; make it a priority.**

# Day 287

***" There are things that you say that you hate now, but you may end up doing tomorrow."***

*"For the good that I would I do not: but the evil which I would not, that I do. Now, if I do that, I would not; it is no more I that do it, but sin that dwelleth in me"(* Romans 7:19-20).

Do you ever find yourself doing something that you are not supposed to do? This is a reality that we can change or refrain from doing. Even though we are humans, and the flesh may want to present itself and seek after its own way. We must know that we are supposed to be led by the Spirit. Being led by the Spirit is not an automatic thing. It's not like a child controlling a remote control car. You are human and your flesh will oppose the things of the flesh. What do you do in these circumstances?

You have to now make a conscious decision that denies the flesh of its desires. The desires of the flesh can be very strong but as you stay in God, you will become more sensitive to the Spirit of God and you will know when He wants to lead you.

**For Contemplation:**

1. Assess your actions daily, take account of any mistake you made and learn from it. Also repent if you need to.

**NOTES:**

________________________________________________

________________________________________________

________________________________________________

**Prayer changes things and people; make it a priority.**

# Day 288

***" Too many people have lost their way because of bread."***

*"Jesus answered them and said, Verily, verily, I say unto you, Ye seek me, not because ye saw the miracles, but because ye did eat of the loaves, and were filled. Labour not for the meat which perisheth, but for that meat which endureth unto everlasting life, which the Son of man shall give unto you: for him hath God the Father sealed"* (John 6:26-27).

Jesus is forthright when it comes to telling the truth. He blatantly told the people that the reason they were following Him was because they got food and were filled. The truth is, many people are just seeking God because of what they can get physically get from Him. They were not seeking the spiritual things and the truth that Jesus had to offer, but rather they sought more after the things of the natural that can easily be destroyed.

Some people have made vows to God that if He delivered them from a certain situation, they would serve Him. The same people who got delivered forget this promise to God and continue to live in sin. Others receive physical things from God, but because of greed, they focus more on what they can get rather than pleasing God, and eventually, they drift away from the presence of God and more towards the presents.

**For Contemplation:**

1. Why are you following Christ? Though we are to ask for

whatever we need, a relationship with Him and our salvation is more important.

NOTES:

---

---

---

**Prayer changes things and people; make it a priority.**

# Day 289

***" When God blesses you, ensure you that you clothe yourself with more humility to handle what He gave you."***

*Put on, therefore, as the elect of God, holy and beloved, bowels of mercies, kindness, humbleness of mind, meekness, longsuffering"* (Colossians 3:12).

As we are the chosen people of God, we must be clothed with humility. As we adorn ourselves with clothes daily, we should be wrapped in humility. When God blesses us with physical things, it is possible for pride to sneak into our hearts. We must guard our hearts from falling into this trap of the enemy. Humility will keep you in the presence of God. If you seek the presence of God, then He will always bless you.

For Contemplation:

1. Remain humble in the midst of your blessings. Use your blessings to be a blessing to others and glorify God.

NOTES:

---

---

---

**Prayer changes things and people; make it a priority.**

# Day 290

***"When you understand that your worship is a weapon, you will learn to use it more often."***

*"Blessed be the Lord my strength which teacheth my hands to war, and my fingers to fight"* (Psalm 144:1).

As your hands are lifted and waved before the Lord, not only do they symbolize adoration and surrender to God, but it can be a powerful weapon. As you wave your hands it can be used to confuse the plans of the enemy. Your worship can confound the enemy and put their plans in disarray. You are not physically fighting a war but as you lift your hands to your Strength, God will fight on your behalf and destroy every plan of the wicked against you.

For Contemplation:

1. What is the importance of worship? Make it your lifestyle.
2. How often do you worship? Make an effort to worship not only at church but in every situation.

NOTES:

______________________________________________

______________________________________________

______________________________________________

**Prayer changes things and people; make it a priority.**

# Day 291

***" Persons who speak bitter words, send arrows in secret."***

*"Who whet their tongue like a sword, and bend their bows to shoot their arrows, even bitter words:*(Psalm 64:3).

The bitter words are synonymous with arrows. Arrows are aerial weapons that are launched by being pulled back in a bow and released. Archers are not located within the battle, but they are strategically positioned at an unseen position. Archers shoot in secret. People who speak bitter words may not always say them in your presence.

However, do not be alarmed, you have the shield of faith. God also has His arrows that will fight for you. *"But God shall shoot at them with an arrow; suddenly shall they be wounded"* (Psalm 64:7 ). God will protect you from all the enemy's devices and weapons. We should be careful that our words do not become arrows against people. We should not speak words that will destroy a person's character or cause them harm. The Lord will fight for us; we only need to arm ourselves with His word and be still. We are armed, but we do not necessarily engage in physical war.

**For Contemplation:**

1. As you pray and cancel all negative words spoken against you, be mindful not to speak any against others.

**NOTES:**

________________________________________

________________________________________

________________________________________

**Prayer changes things and people; make it a priority.**

# Day 292

***" The grace from God cushions the hardness you go through."***

*"I will both lay me down in peace, and sleep: for thou, Lord, only makest*

*me dwell in safety"* (Psalm 4:8).

When you have grace from God, you will rest even in times of hardship. When hardships come, God will comfort you. You won't feel the hardness as much as you should because the grace of God will 'soften the blow'. His grace will take you through.

**For Contemplation:**

1. Name a character in the Bible for whom the grace of God spoke. What was his/her story?

**NOTES:**

__________________________________________________________

__________________________________________________________

__________________________________________________________

**Prayer changes things and people; make it a priority.**

# Day 293

***" The church today has to be the 'Shadrach, Meshack and Abednego' of the 21st century."***

*"Nebuchadnezzar, we are not careful to answer thee in this matter. If it be so, our God whom we serve is able to deliver us from the burning fiery furnace, and he will deliver us out of thine hand, O king. But if not, be it known unto thee, O king, that we will not serve thy gods, nor worship the golden image which thou hast set up"* (Daniel 3:16-18).

The defiance that the three Hebrew men had in this scripture, should be within us as Christians. We must stand up for God. We must develop the tenacity to serve God with all our minds and hearts, to the point where if our lives are being jeopardized, we will still stand.

There will come times when we will have to decide

whether we will stand for the truth of God or bow to the lies of this world. In this time, when even the church is being compromised, we must recognize truth and stand for truth. The end times are here and there will be a great fall away from the faith. We all need to be strong so that we will deny the lies and look to Jesus. Do not compromise your faith with the immorality of the world?

**For Contemplation:**

1. Are you a soldier for Christ? Can you choose Christ in a situation that threatens your life?

**NOTES:**

______________________________________________

______________________________________________

______________________________________________

**Prayer changes things and people; make it a priority.**

# Day 294

***" There are things you need to do to prove loyalty."***

*"If ye love me, keep my commandments"*(John 14:15).

We show our loyalty to God by the actions we do. We are to love God with all our hearts, mind and soul. God gives us commandments that help to guide our lives in a way that is pleasing to Him. Loyalty to God makes you do things that He requires of you, rather than what you think He wants.

In older times, persons were loyal to their kings or queens. They were loyal to the point where they would put their lives on the line in battle. They would fight for their country and pledge allegiance to their sovereign rulers.

**For Contemplation:**

1. How do you show your loyalty to God?

**NOTES:**

______________________________________________

______________________________________________

______________________________________________

**Prayer changes things and people; make it a priority.**

# Day 295

***" The 'slow' has a chance to win."***

*"I returned, and saw under the sun, that the race is not to the swift, nor the battle to the strong, neither yet bread to the wise, nor yet riches to men of understanding, nor yet favour to men of skill; but time and chance happeneth to them all"* (Ecclesiastes 9:11).

The race is not for the swift. Nor the battle for the strong. Normally in the Olympics, the fastest athletes are chosen to represent their country. However, the Bible gives us another perspective on this. Even though we want to put the fastest and the strongest in the race, the Bible says the race is not for the swift. This means then the 'slow' has a chance to win.

God levels the playing field. The mercy of God is for everyone, God is not partial. The instrument that God uses to level the playing field is seasons, chance and opportunity. They happen to all. It is not only for children of God, but everyone. The rain falls on the just and the unjust. It is not because you are good, that God blesses you. He blesses you because He chooses to do so. There are persons who were not born into a wealthy family, and there are some children that may have challenges to learn. This does not mean they have no chance to be blessed by God. They can also get a chance to kick the ball on the playing field.

**For Contemplation:**

1. Find a story in the Bible that demonstrates Ecclesiastes 9:11.

**NOTES:**

___

___

___

**Prayer changes things and people; make it a priority.**

# Day 296

***" We have not been cultured to look for miracles/blessings everyday."***

*"Blessed be the Lord, who daily loadeth us with benefits, even the God of our salvation. Selah"* (Psalm 68:19).

The Lord gives us benefits daily. When we think of the word load, we think of something heavy, and so everyday God loads us with His benefits. We should expect to see the hand of God on our lives in tangibly ways every day. We should not expect God to bless us seldomly or when we are in dire need of a miracle. We should look for His blessings every day. God's best is not miracles, but rather blessings.

As you get up in the morning, speak into your day and ask God to set things in order so that you will receive the daily benefits that He has for you.

**For Contemplation:**

1. How were you blessed yesterday? Speak the blessings you want to manifest today.

**NOTES:**

___

___

___

**Prayer changes things and people; make it a priority.**

# Day 297

***" God wants to push you to birth something new."***

*"That ye put off concerning the former conversation the old man, which is corrupt according to the deceitful lusts; And be renewed in the spirit of your mind; And that ye put on the new man, which after God is created in righteousness and true holiness"*(Ephesians 4:22-24).

God always wants the best for His children. He wants us to enjoy all the benefits and blessings He has prepared for us. There are seasons He wants you to push to get to another level. God will place something in you that needs to be birthed. You are the medium that God chose to bring forth something here on earth; and He is the one who will give you the strength to bring forth your purpose.

**For Contemplation:**

1. Are you willing to push for another level to birth something new? Never be complacent in God. There is always more to achieve.

**NOTES:**

______________________________________________

______________________________________________

______________________________________________

**Prayer changes things and people; make it a priority.**

# Day 298

***" When you pray about something and you do not have peace, do not do it."***

*"Be careful for nothing; but in everything by prayer and supplication*

*with thanksgiving let your requests be made known unto God. And the peace of God, which passeth all understanding, shall keep your hearts and minds through Christ Jesus"* (Philippians 4: 6-7).

Peace paves the way for your decisions. When you have a decision to make, if you do not have peace concerning the decision you want to make, then it is advisable not to do it. The peace of God comes when God agrees with your decision.

God should be in control of your life, and His Spirit should lead us in the decisions that we have to make. We should not try to do things in our own strength, but we must rely on the wisdom of God. The wisdom of God is freely given to us, if we ask God for it (James 1:5). In everything we do, we need the wisdom of God. No matter how simple we may think it is, if we practise to ask God for wisdom in all things, we will have peace in our decisions.

**For Contemplation:**

1. As you seek God about the decisions you make in your daily life, if you are not at peace after praying about the matter then do not carry it out. The peace of God shall keep your heart and mind.

**NOTES:**

____________________________________________

____________________________________________

____________________________________________

**Prayer changes things and people; make it a priority**

# Day 299

***" The devil knows the thoughts that can affect your reality."***

*"Casting down imaginations, and every high thing that exalteth itself against the knowledge of God, and bringing into captivity every thought*

*to the obedience of Christ"* (2 Corinthians 10:5).

The devil can infiltrate our mind with thoughts that can cause you to doubt God. These thoughts will cause us to create a reality that does not belong to us. As soon as these thoughts enter, tear them down and speak the word of God over your mind. These thoughts can affect how you view life, and will cause you to miss what God has for you.

**For Contemplation:**

1. Whenever doubtful thoughts or thoughts that go against the word of God enters your mind, rebuke them. The Word says we are to resist the devil and he will flee.

**NOTES:**

________________________________________

________________________________________

________________________________________

**Prayer changes things and people; make it a priority.**

# Day 300

***" It is important to ask God for the grace to receive the Word of God."***

*"But the natural man receiveth not the things of the Spirit of God: for they are foolishness unto him: neither can he know them, because they are spiritually discerned"* (1 Corinthians 2:14).

The Word of God has to be received through and by the Spirit. Our flesh will not receive revelation from the scriptures, because God does not communicate with our flesh. The things of the Spirit are communicated through the spirit to your spirit.

Therefore, ask God to give you understanding of what He

wants to reveal to you through His Word. If you do not discern the Word spiritually, then you may miss the essence of what God is saying to you specifically. Our spirits must always be in sync with God's Spirit, so that you will receive and understand God's voice to you in that season.

**For Contemplation:**

1. Pray that your spirit be synced with God's spirit. Meditate on His word and seek revelation.

**NOTES:**

---

---

---

**Prayer changes things and people; make it a priority.**

# Day 301

---

***" We have the ability to know the thoughts of God."***

---

*"For who hath known the mind of the Lord, that He may instruct him? but we have the mind of Christ." (*1 Corinthians 2:16 ).

The mind of Christ in us allows us to be connected to the thoughts of God. As you exercise the mind of Christ in you there are thoughts that come to us, but how do we know that they are from God? The thoughts that we have can come from God, the devil or from our own selves.

The nature of our thoughts can be determined by what they lead us to do or how they make us feel. If the thoughts lead you to commit actions that are not pleasing to God, then the thoughts did not originate from Him. Certain thoughts as they bombard the mind, can conjure emotions. If thoughts lead you into a period of despair and hopelessness, they did not come from God. This is the reason why we should tear them down, and replace them with the word of God that grants peace.

As you spend time in the presence of God, you will know His voice. The more you know His voice and His heart, the more you will hear God speaking. When God speaks, you are hearing what He is thinking.

**For Contemplation:**

1. Spend time in the presence of God. Read your Bible, fast, pray and go to church to fellowship and hear the Word. Make notes of what you think God is saying to you. Learn His voice.

**NOTES:**

______________________________________________

______________________________________________

______________________________________________

**Prayer changes things and people; make it a priority.**

# Day 302

***" When you give, you don't have to pray to God for money."***

*"He that hath pity upon the poor lendeth unto the LORD; And that which he hath given will He pay him again"* (Proverbs 19:17 ).

The Bible has principles that should guide us in our daily living. These principles help us to receive the fullness of God's promises. If we follow the principles and laws of God, then it can eliminate us having to go to God in prayer about it.

The scripture says that if you have pity on the poor, other translations say "if you give to the poor, you lend to God." When you lend to someone, the person is now obligated to give back to you. Therefore, as you give to the poor, God will give back to you. These principles that God clearly wrote for His children, are being followed by those who are not His and some are doing it more than us. They understand the principles of God and its benefits, even though they do not belong to God.

Learn to honour God, by giving. Ask God to tell you how

you can give to the poor. The times you ask for money, try to do what He commands you to do.

**For Contemplation:**

1. Don't live life for yourself only. Practice the principle of giving. When God blesses you, be a blessing to others.

**NOTES:**

---

---

---

**Prayer changes things and people; make it a priority.**

# Day 303

---

***" Your dream-life is warfare and you must win."***

---

*"And the multitude of all the nations that fight against Ariel, even all that fight against her and her munition, and that distress her, shall be as a dream of a night vision. It shall even be as when an hungry man dreameth, and, behold, he eateth; but he awaketh, and his soul is empty: or as when a thirsty man dreameth, and, behold, he drinketh; but he awaketh, and, behold, he is faint, and his soul hath appetite: so shall the multitude of all the nations be, that fight against mount Zion"*
( Isaiah 29:7-8).

You have to contend for your dreams. The devil will try to make you forget your dreams, especially if they are important to warn you about your destiny. You should never be satisfied or nonchalant when you cannot remember your dreams. Dreams are your eyes and ears in the realms of the spirit. Dreams will give you prayer points. As dreams are a guide to life, you can know what to pray and how to pray based on the revelation of your dreams.

Before going to sleep, ask God to cover your dream life and reveal what He wants to without any hindrance. Pray that the enemy will not steal your dreams.

**For Contemplation:**

1. Ask God in prayer to cover you dream life. Forbid those that come in the night season from capturing your dreams. Pray for remembrance and always pray concerning what you have dreamt.

**NOTES:**

________________________________________

________________________________________

________________________________________

**Prayer changes things and people; make it a priority.**

# Day 304

***"People who are rebellious look like witches in the spirit."***

*"For rebellion is as the sin of witchcraft, and stubbornness is as iniquity and idolatry. Because thou hast rejected the word of the LORD, he hath also rejected thee from being king"*( 1 Samuel 15:23 ).

The Bible states that rebellion is likened unto the sin of witchcraft. This means that anyone who rebels against the word and principles of God, is in the same category as a witch. We have to be cognizant of when we step outside of God's Word so that we do not fall in the category of being rebellious.

**For Contemplation:**

1. Find two characters in the Bible who were rebellious. How did God deal with them?

**NOTES:**

________________________________________

________________________________________

________________________________________

**Prayer changes things and people; make it a priority.**

# Day 305

***" When a negative thought comes and you reject it, think of a thought to replace it."***

*"Whatsoever you shall bind on earth shall be bound in heaven; and whatsoever you shall loose on earth shall be loosed in heaven (Matthew 18:18).*

When negative thoughts come to plague our minds we should reject them and tear them down. We may always remember to reject and tear down the thought, but we must also remember to fill the gap we cause in the realm of the spirit. We need to replace the negative thoughts with the thoughts of God. We can find these thoughts in His Word. When we bind things here on earth, we should also remember to loose what we desire to see. When we speak here on earth, heaven hears and responds accordingly. Your words help to build your destiny. You are responsible to ensure that heaven has something to respond to and work on your behalf.

**For Contemplation:**

1. Based on the words you speak what does your destiny look like?
2. Don't allow negative thoughts to cause you to sin.
3. Don't dwell on negative thoughts. Rebuke them and replace them with a worship song or scripture.

**NOTES:**

**Prayer changes things and people; make it a priority.**

# Day 306

***" Thoughts and words belong to the spirit realm, but actions belong to the physical realm."***

*"For verily I say unto you, That whosoever shall say unto this mountain, Be thou removed, and be thou cast into the sea; and shall not doubt in his heart, but shall believe that those things which he says shall come to pass; he shall have whatsoever he says." (Mark 11:23).*

Speaking is the action that demonstrates man's dominion here on earth. The words you speak are the products of your thoughts. Your thoughts are formed with words that are inaudible in the physical realm, but they can be powerful in the spiritual realm. When thoughts are present, actions will follow. If you think something, there is the possibility of seeing it come to pass.

**For Contemplation:**

1. Your thoughts are important, which is why God thinks of peace and not evil towards us. As the lord doeth, so should we think peaceful thoughts towards ourselves and others and not of evil.

**.NOTES:**

---

---

---

**Prayer changes things and people; make it a priority.**

# Day 307

***" If you are having a problem in life, find an appropriate scripture and declare it over your situation."***

*"Thou shalt also decree a thing, and it shall be established unto thee: And the light shall shine upon thy ways"* (Job 22:28).

There is nothing new under the sun. Therefore, the Bible has a scripture for everything. The Bible is filled with declarations that we can speak over our situations, and it is filled with wisdom that informs us how to behave and live. As we speak the promises of God over our life, we will see them come to pass.

**For Contemplation:**

1. It is wise to use God's word to Him. God will always keep His promises.

**NOTES:**

____________________________________________

____________________________________________

____________________________________________

**Prayer changes things and people; make it a priority.**

# Day 308

***"We can fall short of the glory of God, but grace is there to catch us."***

*"For all have sinned, and come short of the glory of God; being justified freely by his grace through the redemption that is in Christ Jesus"* (Romans 3:23 - 24).

We are not saved because of our good deeds and character, but we are saved because God loves us. His grace brings us to repentance so that we can be joint-heirs with Christ Jesus. We must be grateful to God for His grace that He willingly bestows upon us. He does not give it sparingly, but He saturates us with grace. His grace covers a multitude of sins, however, we should not take His grace for granted. The vastness of grace aligns with the infinite character of God. It goes on from generation to generation. Our duty is to continue to serve Him and He will sustain us.

**For Contemplation:**

1. We can do nothing to deserve God's love, goodness and blessings. Having a grateful heart will help us to appreciate what God is doing for us. Sing praises to His name. Magnify Him with your words and actions.

**NOTES:**

______________________________________________

______________________________________________

______________________________________________

**Prayer changes things and people; make it a priority.**

# Day 309

***"Ask God to increase your perception of Him."***

*"For God speaketh once, yea twice, yet man perceiveth it not. In a dream, in a vision of the night, when deep sleep falleth upon men, in slumberings upon the bed; Then He openeth the ears of men, and sealeth their instruction"* ( Job 33:14-16).

Our sensitivity to God needs to be at a certain level, that when God speaks to us, we know His voice. Doubt will not be present in us because we know Him. God speaks to us when we are conscious and awake. However, based on the scripture, God waits until we sleep to speak through dreams, because men perceive not. Perceive means to discern, or to become aware of. We need to be aware of God when we are awake and when we are asleep. He is always speaking and so we must be on the lookout for what He is saying within that moment. We should anticipate hearing God's voice, until it becomes innate to desire His voice at all times.

**For Contemplation:**

1. After you pray, spend quiet time with God to perceive what He is saying. Intently listen for the voice of God. When He gives you dreams pray concerning them. Desire to hear from God.

**NOTES:**

______________________________________________

______________________________________________

______________________________________________

**Prayer changes things and people; make it a priority.**

# Day 310

***" Your actions are a response to your act of hearing."***

*"But be ye doers of the word, and not hearers only, deceiving your own selves. For if any be a hearer of the word, and not a doer, he is like unto a man beholding his natural face in a glass:"* James 1:22-23

As you hear the Word of God, you are expected to respond to it. Your response to the word heard signifies your belief or unbelief. If you say you believe in the Word of God; as you hear it, your actions should match your belief. You cannot hear the Word of God and still be the same person with the same mindset. The Word of God should resound in your spirit and cause you to act differently. You now believe in God's Word. Therefore, your life should reflect that your trust is in God.

**For Contemplation:**

1. Are you a deceiver? Do you follow all that God asks of you or you pick which principles to apply to your life? As you study the Word of God, apply it to your life and do what He asks of you. Otherwise, you will be a deceiver.

NOTES:

---

---

---

**Prayer changes things and people; make it a priority.**

# Day 311

***"The Blood of Jesus became the cheat code for those who accepted salvation."***

*"For sin shall not have dominion over you: for ye are not under the law, but under grace. What then? shall we sin, because we are not under the law, but under grace? God forbid"* (Romans 6:14-15).

Salvation allowed us to be free from the law of sin that judges the world. We are in the world, but we are not of the world, because we are no longer under the law of sin. The shedding of Jesus' blood allowed us to have a different route from those who don't know Jesus and reject Him. We are under the law of grace. God's standards are extremely high, as we can see in the Old Testament. Remember the death of Uzzah? We may believe that we are living by God's standards, but in truth, we are living by God's grace.

We are supposed to be of clean hands and pure hearts, if we want to see God. Jesus Christ was our sacrifice and He made it easier for mankind. We can choose between the path of sin and death or the path of eternal life.

**For Contemplation:**

1. Under the law of grace, we can confess our sins, forsake them, and receive mercy. When you repent of your sins, don't go back. Work out your salvation each day with fear and trembling.

NOTES:

---

---

---

**Prayer changes things and people; make it a priority.**

# Day 312

---

*"You cannot value people by their possessions."*

---

*"And he said unto them, Take heed, and beware of covetousness: for a man's life consisteth not in the abundance of the things which he possesseth"* (Luke 12:15).

We can look at the possessions that people have and based on what we physically see, we conclude that this person is blessed more than persons who may not have many possessions. However, Jesus tells us not to place value on someone's life because of what they have. Earthly possessions can be a symbol of God's mercy and goodness, yes, but these do not necessarily reflect the person's relationship with God.

In the Bible, Jesus tells the parable of a rich man who stored up grains and food. He even built bigger storehouses to keep the abundance of what he had for himself. He had so much, but instead of giving or sharing, he kept it for himself to eat and to be merry. However, in the night, God came to him and said his soul was required from him. In simple terms, he was going to die, and the Lord asked him, who will these stored-up goods belong to then? They cannot go where he is going.

We should remember that the Lord sends the rain on the just and the unjust. Therefore, we cannot use good things or even bad things to judge a person's position in Christ. Instead, we should use the fruits we see, to determine the truth of the lips.

**For Contemplation:**

1. How should we value people? Meditate on Matthew 19:16 – 30.

**NOTES:**

______________________________________________

______________________________________________

______________________________________________

**Prayer changes things and people; make it a priority.**

# Day 313

***" Some of the laws that exist originated from God."***

*"Let every soul be subject unto the higher powers. For there is no power but of God: the powers that be are ordained of God. Whosoever therefore resisteth the power, resisteth the ordinance of God: and they that resist shall receive to themselves damnation"* (Romans 13:1-2).

Have you ever seen someone swear on the Bible as they enter a courtroom to testify or have you seen a President of the United States resting their hand on the Bible taking the oath as they are sworn into the position?

There are many laws that originate or connect with the principles of the Bible. God is the only power, and therefore, those that we see in positions of authority over a certain region were ordained by Him. This is why God instructs us to obey those who are set in authority. If you resist or rebel, then you must be prepared to deal with the consequences. In order for us to have a peaceful life, we must pray for our leaders.

**For Contemplation:**

1. Timothy tells us to make supplications, prayers, intercessions, and thanksgiving for all men, for kings, and for all who are in authority. Pray for the leaders of the world, your country, your

community, your work, your church, and your family. Pray for all who are in authority, whether formally or informally.

**NOTES:**

______________________________________________

______________________________________________

______________________________________________

**Prayer changes things and people; make it a priority.**

# Day 314

***"Persons make their commandments into doctrines."***

***"Howbeit in vain do they worship me, Teaching for doctrines the commandments of men"*** (Mark 7:7).

Some doctrines are preached and kept in some churches that really did not originate from God. Some have made it a requirement for persons to be a part of their congregation and if they do not uphold them they are treated as outcasts. For example, many Adventists proclaim that those who worship on Sunday will go to hell, but is this biblically correct? Is there a scripture in the Bible that supports this? We have to be careful of the doctrines being enforced that push us further into the bondage of religion, rather than pushing us into the presence of God.

**For Contemplation:**

1. Are your beliefs found in the Bible?
2. Make it a habit to verify the word shared in church with scripture. Make it your responsibility to prove that the person sharing is wrong or right.

NOTES:

---

---

---

**Prayer changes things and people; make it a priority.**

# Day 315

***"There is a generation that will bring change into existence."***

*"This shall be written for the generation to come: and the people which shall be created shall praise the Lord"* (Psalm 102:18).

Abraham's generation carried the promise of God. Then from Abraham to David, David carried the kingly anointing. After David, there came Zedekiah, and Zedekiah rebelled against the word of God and caused his generation to enter into bondage. However, Christ came and there came the Christian generation. It takes one man to change a generation. We are called Christians because we are supposed to look like Christ.

Therefore, we have the anointing of Christ. We carry the anointing that can change our generation. Before Jesus Christ was born, the Jews had to go to the temple to make sacrifice for their sin, but after Jesus Christ came, we do not need to sacrifice any animals to get forgiveness. Christ died for us so that we could be saved. Jesus qualified us, and now we are joint heirs with Him. We will get the things we do not deserve.

**For Contemplation:**

1. What was the promise of God to Abraham's generation?

NOTES:

______________________________________________

______________________________________________

______________________________________________

**Prayer changes things and people; make it a priority.**

# Day 316

***" You are now engrafted into the family tree of God."***

*"And if some of the branches be broken off, and thou, being a wild olive tree, wert graffed in among them, and with them partakest of the root and fatness of the olive tree"*(Romans 11:17).

We were engrafted to the tree of God. God allowed us to be a part of His family; we were not born as people of God. The Israelites were His chosen people on earth. However, God, with His love for not just the Israelites but also us Gentiles, gave us a chance of life. We are now engrafted to the family tree of God. We were the wild olive tree and so we can now be partakers of the grace and love of God. When we are a part of the lineage, we are a part of the legacy.

**For Contemplation:**

1. Let us not waste this opportunity that God has given us to be like Christ and be perfect in Him.

NOTES:

______________________________________________

______________________________________________

______________________________________________

**Prayer changes things and people; make it a priority.**

# Day 317

***" Hope can be affected by man, but my faith can only be affected by me."***

*"And Jesus said unto them, Because of your unbelief: for verily I say unto you, If ye have faith as a grain of mustard seed, ye shall say unto this mountain, Remove hence to yonder place; and it shall remove; and nothing shall be impossible unto you"* (Matthew 17:20).

The changes you want to see in your life, depend on your faith in God. Even if your faith is as small as a mustard seed, you can see the impossible being done in your life. When you have hope, this can be altered by you but also by the words of others. However, if you have faith in God, nothing external can affect it. The words or actions of others around you have no power to affect your faith. Your faith is dependent on your relationship with God. The more you get to know God, the more your faith in Him increases. You trust Him, hence, you know He will do what He says He will. Your hope means that you have a belief that you will get something, but you also have a 'just in case' it doesn't happen. Faith eliminates every doubt.

**For Contemplation:**

1. Do you possess faith or hope?
2. When you ask for something, do you have a backup plan, or are you believing wholeheartedly because there is no other way?

**NOTES:**

______________________________________________

______________________________________________

______________________________________________

**Prayer changes things and people; make it a priority.**

# Day 318

***" If you are a believer of God, you have some form of immunity to any sickness."***

*" Who His own self bare our sins in His own body on the tree, that we, being dead to sins, should live unto righteousness: by whose stripes ye were healed"* (1 Peter 2:24).

As Jesus' body was scourged for you and me, we have immunity to diseases. As His flesh was ripped, our bodies can be repaired and restored if it is affected by any disease. He took the stripes for us, so that when we call on His name and believe we are healed; it is done. As Christians, we should have a certain level of resistance to diseases.

**For Contemplation:**

1. Our bodies are the temples of the living God and Isaiah tells us with His stripes we are healed. Sickness have no place in our bodies especially the infirmities of Satan.
2. Never claim sickness; only claim your health.

**NOTES:**

______________________________________________

______________________________________________

______________________________________________

**Prayer changes things and people; make it a priority.**

# Day 319

***" Learn to meet God's fire and allow His fire to meet you."***

*"I indeed baptize you with water unto repentance: but he that cometh after me is mightier than I, whose shoes I am not worthy to bear: he shall baptize you with the Holy Ghost, and with fire"( Matthew 3:11 ).*

Ask the Lord to give you His fire. Let us examine John. According to John 5:35, he was described as a burning and shining light. He was a light that lit the way for the coming of Jesus and prepared the people for his coming. He never lost his zeal, he knew his assignment even though he himself was also waiting for the Messiah to come. We should be on fire for God. I know we have heard this, but our light must shine for God so that others will be attracted and come to glorify our God too. We must not be dim today and bright tomorrow, the language used to describe John was present continuous. Meaning you should always be burning for God. Your light must be shining.

The light is what bears witness of your relationship with God. As Jesus was baptized, "And Jesus, when He was baptized, went up straightway out of the water and, lo, the heavens were opened unto Him, and He saw the Spirit of God descending like a dove, and lighting upon Him" (Matthew 3:16) . The light in John bore witness with the light that rested on Jesus. Light knows light, therefore, ensure that the light of Jesus can be seen by everyone around you.

**For Contemplation:**

1. Are you burning for God, or is your light flickering? Those around you should know that you serve a great big, wonderful God on good days and bad days.

**NOTES:**

______________________________________________

______________________________________________

______________________________________________

**Prayer changes things and people; make it a priority.**

# Day 320

***"Your reactions suggest an underlying cause."***

*"And he called the multitude, and said unto them, Hear, and understand: not that which goeth into the mouth defileth a man; but that which cometh out of the mouth, this defileth a man"* (Matthew 15: 10 - 11).

This scripture suggests that what comes from within someone defiles them, and not external factors. Therefore, our actions are as a result of what really is within. We must know what we have on our inside so that we can break it from our lives. As we break it from our lives, the Spirit of God should be inside to begin to work in us. Changing our attitudes, or personalities, our bad habits, or ideologies; and replacing them with His ways.

**For Contemplation:**

1. What comes out of your mouth when you are frustrated?
2. Renew your mind, spend the time to form new habits as you are a new creature in Christ. New wine cannot be poured into old wine skin.

**NOTES:**

______________________________________________

______________________________________________

______________________________________________

**Prayer changes things and people; make it a priority.**

# Day 321

***"Do not give anyone your heart."***

*"Not rendering evil for evil, or railing for railing: but contrariwise blessing; knowing that ye are thereunto called, that ye should inherit a blessing"* (1 Peter 3:9).

There are times when people do things that hurt or offend us, and we may react negatively or godly to their actions, which leads to consequences. In these instances, flesh may want to be seen and validated, but sometimes it is best to overlook an offense. It is best not to give way to this spirit because it can lead to us behaving in ungodly ways that displease God. Do not give anyone the access to rule over your heart; do not allow the actions of others to cause you to behave in ways that grieve the Holy Spirit. Remember that you wrestle not against flesh and blood, but against principalities, wickedness in high places, and evil spirits. It is not about the person, understand that there is a spirit at play, a spirit that is trying to destroy relationships, and we must not give ourselves over to being vessels for these spirits that are trying to cause us to err in the face of God. God says love them that curse you, and love your neighbour as yourself. He did not say to love only those you want to love. God's love is for everyone and so should your love too.

Sometimes, we even want to go to God about someone in prayer,but remember that we are all His creations, all are His sons and daughters. It makes no sense to stir up mischief and bring it before God. He already gave you instructions, which is to love them and live peaceably with them. We easily forget this law of God, because in any heated moment our flesh becomes louder than the voice of God.We allow others' actions to ruin our hearts and character. It is important for us to renew our minds daily with the word of God. If we do not, we will realize that our flesh will be renewed and strengthened. Remember, flesh cannot be in the presence of God.

**For Contemplation:**

1. Reflect on Luke 6:29. If someone has done evil towards you pray that they will turn their heart to God and repent. Don't allow anyone's actions to get in your heart.

NOTES:

________________________________________

________________________________________

________________________________________

**Prayer changes things and people; make it a priority.**

# Day 322

***"Your God-destiny completes you."***

*"For I know the thoughts that I think toward you, saith the LORD, thoughts of peace, and not of evil, to give you an expected end"* (Jeremiah 29:11).

Your purpose is not in your job or in your skills. Your purpose is the divine mandate that God assigned to you before your very existence in this realm. Therefore, the gifts, talents and skills you developed over time here on earth does not define your purpose. Your purpose is the plan God has for you. It is not based on your limitations, nor your skills. It is based on the will of God. The plans of God for you gives you an expected end, this means it completes you. Once you know the will of God for your life, you know your purpose and then you will begin to live a life based on what you know. Your gift, talents and skills aid in your purpose, but they are not your purpose.

Ask God to reveal His plan and purpose for your life. Listen to His instructions and obey Him.

**For Contemplation:**

1. What is your purpose? What is the will of God for your life?

NOTES:

---

---

---

**Prayer changes things and people; make it a priority.**

# Day 323

***"If you wait on the Lord you don't have to force. If you wait you won't be torn."***

*"The LORD is good unto them that wait for Him, To the soul that seeketh Him"*( Lamentations 3:25).

They that wait on the Lord shall renew their strength. Waiting on the Lord does not deplete you; instead you will be renewed. You do not have to force yourself to do anything, you need to know that God will come through for you.

**For Contemplation:**

1. There is strength in waiting. While you wait on God, praise Him, glorify His name, be patient, your season will come.

NOTES:

---

---

---

**Prayer changes things and people; make it a priority.**

# Day 324

***" Satan is after your peace."***

*"Be sober, be vigilant; because your adversary the devil, as a roaring lion, walketh about, seeking whom he may devour"* (1 Peter 5:8).

Do not allow the devil to rob you of your peace. Your peace is an intangible fruit of the Spirit of God in you. Peace will keep your mind focused on God even in the most chaotic situations. Your mind is a very common place for the devil to fight you. Once he infiltrates your mind, your peace is compromised and once that is compromised the stability of your mind is.

You need to guard yourself against the devices of the devil. You need to resist him and he will flee. You need to declare that your mind is not a playground for the devil. Keep your mind on God and He will keep you in perfect peace (Isaiah 26:3).

**For Contemplation:**

1. Spend five minutes to pray against any attack of the enemy on your mind.

**NOTES:**

---

---

---

**Prayer changes things and people; make it a priority.**

# Day 325

***" God's reality contradicts our reality."***

*"But, beloved, be not ignorant of this one thing, that one day is with the Lord as a thousand years, and a thousand years as one day."* 2 Peter 3:8

God operates on a totally different wavelength than that of our reality. He works according to His own time, not ours. As the scripture says, for God, a day is like a thousand years, and a thousand years is like a day for Him. He is not bound by the limitations of time. He was before time began, and He will be forever when time ends.

**For Contemplation:**

1. God is not limited by time. He is on time, and His divine timing is greater than anything else.

**NOTES:**

______________________________________________

______________________________________________

______________________________________________

**Prayer changes things and people; make it a priority.**

# Day 326

***'You cannot sit back and be comfortable in failure."***

*"For a just man falleth seven times, and riseth up again: But the wicked shall fall into mischief"* (Proverbs 24:16).

How do you react to failure? As a righteous man, resilience is a part of your nature. You cannot be defeated by failure. Every experience of failure is a chance for you to start anew. Start a different way from the last time you tried, and see what works. Do not sit back and allow failure to become a negative outcome for you. Use it to cause a positive change.

**For Contemplation:**

1. Think of something you failed at. Pray to see what God is saying about it. If you believe it is a part of God's plan for

your life apply all that you have learnt so far and try at it again.

**NOTES:**

________________________________________

________________________________________

________________________________________

**Prayer changes things and people; make it a priority.**

# Day 327

***"Jesus already pronounced a blessing on those who will be persecuted for His sake."***

*"Blessed are they which are persecuted for righteousness' sake: for their's is the kingdom of heaven"* (Matthew 5:10 ).

Reaction to persecution may not always be welcoming. People react in different ways, and if you do not have the Spirit of God, your reaction can be displeasing to God. Persecution for the gospel's sake comes with a promise of being blessed and inheriting the kingdom of God.

**For Contemplation:**

1. The blessing does not come without persecution, and persecution for God's sake comes with a promise. Therefore, be encouraged to laugh in the midst of adversities.

**NOTES:**

________________________________________

________________________________________

________________________________________

**Prayer changes things and people; make it a priority.**

# Day 328

*"Try not to say anything ungodly."*

***"But now ye also put off all these; anger, wrath, malice, blasphemy, filthy communication out of your mouth"*** ( Colossians 3:8 ).

When we hear the word ungodly, we think of "bad word". However, it is really any word that is anti-god. They do not belong in the presence of God. Bad words can defile you and alter your character.

**For Contemplation:**

1. Remember life and death is in the power of the tongue.

**NOTES:**

________________________________________

________________________________________

________________________________________

**Prayer changes things and people; make it a priority.**

# Day 329

***" You have to change your mindset in order to rise above the situation."***

*"And be not conformed to this world: but be ye transformed by the renewing of your mind, that ye may prove what is that good, and acceptable, and perfect, will of God"* (Romans 12:2 ).

Your mindset is important for change to happen. If you continually see yourself at the position you are at, then it will be difficult to rise above it. A changed mindset means a changed destiny. You have the power to decide whether the change will be good or bad.

**For Contemplation**

1. What mindset do you need to change to move forward?

**NOTES:**

________________________________________________

________________________________________________

________________________________________________

**Prayer changes things and people; make it a priority.**

# Day 330

***" The natural man does not have the right spirit."***

*"Now we have received, not the spirit of the world, but the spirit which is of God; that we might know the things that are freely given to us of God"*(1 Corinthians 2:12).

Our natural state is without the Spirit of God. The change comes when we receive Him in our hearts and He gives us His Spirit. Now we are the children of God. Our natural man cannot receive the things of God. We must first deny ourselves, subject our flesh and allow Jesus into our hearts. By Him, we are saved, and by His ways, we are changed. When we have the Holy Spirit, we are now more aware of the presence and move of God. As we have the Holy Spirit, we should ensure that our vessels are conducive for Him to dwell in.

**For Contemplation:**

1. Is your vessel conducive for the Holy Spirit to dwell?

**NOTES:**

________________________________________________

________________________________________________

________________________________________________

**Prayer changes things and people; make it a priority.**

# Day 331

***"The wisdom of God can make anyone into a mighty man."***

*"And God gave Solomon wisdom and understanding exceeding much, and largeness of heart, even as the sand that is on the seashore. And Solomon's wisdom excelled the wisdom of all the children of the east country, and all the wisdom of Egypt. For he was wiser than all men; than Ethan the Ezrahite, and Heman, and Chalcol, and Darda, the sons of Mahol: and his fame was in all nations round about"* (1 Kings 4:29-31).

The power of God can transform any mere man into a mighty man. Solomon asked for wisdom, and God caused him to be the wisest person known in history and this wisdom led to him become the wealthiest man to date.

In order for you to be transformed by God, ask Him for the right things. We are tempted to ask God for material things most of the time, but we should also ask Him for wisdom. His wisdom surpasses all human intelligence. Ask God to give you wisdom even in the simplest of situations that you encounter daily. The more you ask Him for it, the more your desire grows and He will freely give it to you. When we ask God for something, do not ask from a selfish point of view. Instead, it should be beneficial to others rather than yourself.

**For Contemplation:**

1. How can the things you pray for benefit those around you?

**NOTES:**

---

---

---

**Prayer changes things and people; make it a priority.**

# Day 332

***" Do not stop believing that God does the extraordinary. He wants to do more than what you expect."***

*"And a certain man lame from his mother's womb was carried, whom they laid daily at the gate of the temple which is called Beautiful, to ask alms of them that entered into the temple; who seeing Peter and John about to go into the temple asked an alms. And Peter, fastening his eyes upon him with John, said, Look on us. And he gave heed unto them, expecting to receive something of them. Then Peter said, Silver and gold have I none; but such as I have give I thee: In the name of Jesus Christ of Nazareth rise up and walk. And he took him by the right hand, and lifted him up: and immediately his feet and ankle bones received strength"* (Acts 3:2-7).

God wants to do more than what your mind can think of asking. His abilities and capabilities are beyond the limitations of this world, and this is where we ought to be. We must believe that God can do more than what we are asking of Him. The lame man was so used to asking for money, and maybe he gave up on the idea of walking again. However, he received more than what he asked , he received his miracle effortlessly.

**For Contemplation:**

1. List five things God has done for you recently.

**NOTES:**

______________________________________________

______________________________________________

______________________________________________

**Prayer changes things and people; make it a priority.**

# Day 333

***" Do not trust God when it is convenient or when you are desperate. Trust Him at all times."***

*"And Jesus said unto them, Because of your unbelief: for verily I say unto you, If ye have faith as a grain of mustard seed, ye shall say unto this mountain, Remove hence to yonder place; and it shall remove; and nothing shall be impossible unto you"* (Matthew 17:20).

Our faith in God should never waver. We should constantly trust in Him and exercise our faith in Him. We are expected to please Him at all times and we cannot please Him without faith. Even if our faith is as small as a mustard seed we can still please Him. We shouldn't go to God only when we are in need. We should show Him that we are not His children only when we need Him to come through for us. We should exercise our trust in Him at all times.

**For Contemplation:**

1. Learn to trust God with everything. Start with the smaller things and watch Him keep His promises. Then, increase as you go along.

**NOTES:**

______________________________________________

______________________________________________

______________________________________________

**Prayer changes things and people; make it a priority.**

# Day 334

***" Many people have length of days, but not quality of life."***

*"What man is he that desireth life, And loveth many days, that he may see good"* (Psalm 34:12)?

Some persons live long, but the joy of the Lord does not fulfill them. As Christians, we should desire to live. We should be grateful for life, not just to live lavishly, but to fulfill the will of God in our lives. We have a reason to live: to please and live for God. Our lives are not for us only, but we are to be a blessing to others.

**For Contemplation:**

1. In what way have you been a blessing to someone recently? Do you believe God is pleased with your actions?

**NOTES:**

______________________________________________

______________________________________________

______________________________________________

**Prayer changes things and people; make it a priority.**

# Day 335

***"You must recognize how frail you are before God."***

*"The sacrifices of God are a broken spirit: A broken and a contrite heart, O God, thou wilt not despise"* (Psalm 51:17).

The Lord requires that we be broken. Broken does not mean crying all the time, or depressed all the time. No, those are not our portions. Instead, we must always know our place in God. He is the Creator, we are the creations. Therefore, we need Him. We are dependent on Him. We cannot live without Him. God knows us, He knows that we are flesh before Him and He knows our limitations. However, we can be made perfect through Him, not because of our own abilities. We are in constant need of God and we are in need of each other.

**For Contemplation:**

1. What are four reasons why you believe you need God?

**NOTES:**

________________________________________________

________________________________________________

________________________________________________

**Prayer changes things and people; make it a priority.**

# Day 336

***"Keep your tongue, know when to speak."***

*"Be ye not as the horse, or as the mule, which have no understanding: Whose mouth must be held in with bit and bridle, lest they come near unto thee"* (Psalm 32:9).

The wisdom of the Lord will teach you when and how to speak. We should not rely on our own emotions to guide our speech. We should rely on the Holy Spirit.

**For Contemplation:**

1. Think of an instance where your mouth got you in trouble. What did you say, and what would you do differently, given the wealth of knowledge you have today?

**NOTES:**

____________________________________________

____________________________________________

____________________________________________

**Prayer changes things and people; make it a priority.**

# Day 337

***" People do not invest in people, they invest in ideas."***

*"And He hath filled him with the spirit of God, in wisdom, in understanding, and in knowledge, and in all manner of workmanship; and to devise curious works, to work in gold, and in silver, and in brass" ( Exodus 35:31*-32).

People do not invest in people, they invest in the ideas of people. They look for people who have solutions to problems that are faced by a wide variety of people. Ask God to give you creative ideas that can help people and be a legacy to future generations.

**For Contemplation:**

1. Spend ten minutes praying to God for witty ideas and inventions. Be sure to execute them when you receive them.

**NOTES:**

____________________________________________

____________________________________________

____________________________________________

**Prayer changes things and people; make it a priority.**

# Day 338

***"The more you make the right decision, the more you deny your flesh."***

*"For they that are after the flesh do mind the things of the flesh; but they that are after the Spirit the things of the Spirit. For to be carnally minded is death; but to be spiritually minded is life and peace. Because the carnal mind is enmity against God: for it is not subject to the law of God, neither indeed can be. So then they that are in the flesh cannot please God"* (Romans 8: 5-8).

As you make the right decisions, God will be glorified in your life. The right decision does not necessarily mean what you think is the right thing to do. The right decisions come from the Spirit of God. Therefore, if you have the spirit of God, He will direct your path. The Bible tells us not to lean on our own understanding, because to you it may seem right, but the end thereof are the ways of death (Proverbs 14:12).

Train your flesh to be subjected to the leading of the Spirit of God. The flesh can be subjected once you direct your mind and will to be changed. After this decision, the Spirit will give you strategies to keep your flesh in check and for Him to live in you. The Spirit of God must dwell within you in order for you to make the right decision. Wisdom originates from God, hence His wisdom should be applied daily to every situation.

**For Contemplation:**

1. Write down every decision you are faced with this month, find scriptures to support the choices you make as you seek the wisdom of God.

**NOTES:**

______________________________

______________________________

______________________________

**Prayer changes things and people; make it a priority.**

# Day 339

***" When a human being makes a covenant, he does not make it for himself only but for his lineage."***

*"And I will make thee exceeding fruitful, and I will make nations of thee, and kings shall come out of thee. And I will establish my covenant between me and thee and thy seed after thee in their generations for an everlasting covenant, to be a God unto thee, and to thy seed after thee"* (Genesis 17:6-7).

In Genesis, God shows us the importance of covenants. He instigated the concept of covenant to man, and He also spoke of the duration of the covenant. Covenants do not only affect one person. Even if the person God initially entered the covenant with died, the laws of the covenant are still in effect in the future generations. When entering a covenant with God, do not think about yourself only, but think of it as a standard that you want to see upheld in your immediate family and the generations to come.

**For Contemplation:**

1. What covenants have you made with God? Have you honoured your covenants? If not, repent and start now.

**NOTES:**

______________________________________________

______________________________________________

______________________________________________

**Prayer changes things and people; make it a priority.**

# Day 340

***"Error does not take away your holiness."***

*"That ye put off concerning the former conversation the old man, which is corrupt according to the deceitful lusts; And be renewed in the spirit of your mind; And that ye put on the new man, which after God is created in righteousness and true holiness"* (Ephesians 4: 22-24).

When we sin, the first thing that comes to our mind is to run. People run from God in the form of not attending church and withdrawing from fellow Christians; but your error does not take away your standing with God. Our errors are known to God, even the ones that we haven't committed yet. This does not cause Him to disregard or reject us because there is the unlimited power of grace.

It is up to us to realize what makes us short of the glory of God, and rely on the power of the Holy Spirit to repent and turn from our wicked ways. Your errors do not cause you to be orphaned by God, He still loves you. However, your errors may not erase the consequences that accompany them. But do not look at these as a final judgment. There is still the time of grace, as there is no repentance in the grave. Repent, learn from your errors and mistakes, and live in the freedom by which Christ has made you free. Do not become entangled in the yoke of bondage anymore, and live in holiness before God.

**For Contemplation:**

1. Find two examples of men or women in the Bible that erred but made it right with God. Who were they? What did they do? How did they make it right? What can you learn from their story?

**NOTES:**

________________________________________________

________________________________________________

________________________________________________

**Prayer changes things and people; make it a priority.**

# Day 341

*" Do not fast unto God with the wrong motives."*

*"... for they disfigure their faces, that they may appear unto men to fast. Verily I say unto you, They have their reward. But thou, when thou fastest, anoint thine head, and wash thy face; That thou appear not unto men to fast, but unto thy Father which is in secret: and thy Father, which seeth in secret, shall reward thee openly"*( Matthew 6:16-18).

Fasting is a sacred action to God. It is a time to cleanse your spirit and to humble your soul. We must ensure that when we fast that God will acknowledge it, if it is with the wrong intention or with the wrong posture of your heart, it will be ignored.

Here are a few benefits of fasting, when done in the right way:

1. It gets rid of pride. Fasting humbles the soul.
2. It looses the bands of wickedness.
3. It undoes heavy burdens.
4. It frees the oppressed.
5. It breaks every yoke.
6. It gives you clarity from God. As your physical emotions and senses are dampened, your spiritual senses are heightened.
7. It causes your enemies to be revealed.
8. Fasting has the power to shift judgement. In 1 Kings 21: 28-29, God shifted the punishment from King Ahab to his son. Ahab was a wicked king and God declared that He would punish Ahab by killing all the male seed. Upon hearing this judgement, Ahab fasted and humbled himself before God, and God did not bring this evil he promised upon Ahab. Instead, he reserved this punishment in the time of his son's days. If God did this for a wicked king, He is more than able to shift judgments on your behalf once you

repent and humble yourself.

9. Fasting transcends generations. You can lay a path for your future generations. By fasting and laying this foundation, your family will be supported by this, and God will remember and save them.

There is power in your fasting, once you have the right motive. Do not abuse this strategy that God has given us.

**For Contemplation:**

1. Be intentional with your fasting; do not be concerned with what you can or cannot consume but rather find more ways to give of yourself and die to flesh.

**NOTES:**

____________________________________________________

____________________________________________________

____________________________________________________

**Prayer changes things and people; make it a priority.**

# Day 342

***" The best place to be, is to be in right standing with God."***

*"For do I now persuade men, or God? or do I seek to please men? for if I yet pleased men, I should not be the servant of Christ"* (Galatians 1:10).

To be in right standing with God should be the ultimate goal for all of us. We should be determined to hear at the end of it all, "Well done, my good and faithful servant" from the mouth of God. Our trophies, accomplishments, and applauses on this earth will not follow us to the final judgement. It will not be used to validate us if we get to reign with Jesus forever.

Pleasing God should be a conscious decision we make every day. As you are about to do or say something, ask yourself.

"Can I do or say this right in front of God? Will He be pleased? The moment we do things that cause us to be in right standing with God, the better our outcomes will be in every area of our lives.

**For Contemplation:**

1. What does it mean to be in right standing with God? Look back at the last 11 months, are you in right standing with Him? If not, it's not too late to repent.

**NOTES:**

______________________________________________

______________________________________________

______________________________________________

**Prayer changes things and people; make it a priority.**

# Day 343

***" Be uncomfortable for a season, to become comfortable for a lifetime."***

*"But the God of all grace, who hath called us unto His eternal glory by Christ Jesus, after that ye have suffered a while, make you perfect, stablish, strengthen, settle you"* (1 Peter 5: 10).

Do you remember that time and chance happen to all? Do you remember that all things will work together for your good. Today I encourage you to look beyond your current situation. Whatever you are faced with in this present moment, look at it through the eyes of God. He alone knows your future, therefore, do not go on predicting and coming up with visions of your future. He is the Way-maker, the Promise-keeper, the Light in every Darkness.

I know whatever you are facing is uncomfortable, but it should build your faith in God. Use the problems you face to build and fortify your faith in God. Give the enemy some confusion to deal with. Stand up and stand strong, God will bring you to a place of rest. Once you are walking upright, and following His principles, the challenges you experience are tests, and one thing about tests, they are temporary. They pop up now and then, but once you do them and pass, you never see the same tests again. They broaden your capacity for knowledge; the broader the capacity, the greater the wisdom. You will breathe the sigh of relief when the tests are over, do not quit now.

**For Contemplation:**

1. Find the story of the woman with the issue of blood. Was the situation comfortable? Did she give up on her breakthrough? What lessons have you learned from the story?

**NOTES:**

______________________________________________

______________________________________________

______________________________________________

**Prayer changes things and people; make it a priority.**

# Day 344

***" If your mind is going in the wrong direction, your faith will go in the wrong direction."***

*"A double-minded man is unstable in all his ways"* (James 1: 8 ).

Your mind is one of the most powerful tools God has given to you. You must learn how to protect it and win the battles that constantly attack you there. It is one of the places where the devil attacks because he cannot get to your thoughts but can influence them. He knows the impact he can have once he gets through to your mind. As Christians, we must fortify our minds with the word of God. Our minds must be filled with thoughts of God, in order to know the thoughts of God we must have a relationship with Him, and we must also read His Word. The words we read in the Bible, that were written by human hands, originated from the mind of God. Once you have this revelation, the promises that are yea and amen are for you and your generation.

You have to get your mind centered and focused on God, if you have the slightest deviation it can have a tremendous impact. The slightest deviation signals to Satan that he can try to send thoughts your way. You must be strong enough to tear them down and subject your thoughts to Christ. You must have the power to resist the devil, and I guarantee you, he will flee. We need to stop this culture of giving the devil fake credit, when he himself has no authority over a child of God. You possess the mind of Christ and He was given all power when He rose again and conquered death, hell and the grave! Hallelujah! He rose and He gave this power to you, so that on this earth you are able to live according to the laws of the Kingdom of God.

Ask God daily to keep your mind stayed on Him, as He will give you perfect peace. Your mind has the ability to center your faith accurately to its target. Do not go off course.

**For Contemplation:**

1. When unwanted thoughts plague your mind, open your mouth and rebuke them. Then, replace the thoughts by meditating on a scripture, listening to worship music, or actively thinking about something else.

**NOTES:**

________________________________________

________________________________________

________________________________________

**Prayer changes things and people; make it a priority.**

# Day 345

***" Hard times produce creative people. Hard-working people produce easy times. Easy times produce lazy people."***

*"I wisdom dwell with prudence and find out knowledge of witty inventions " (Proverbs 8:12).*

The most inventions and creative ideas came about when the world was plunged into a state of chaos, mayhem and fear. Yes, Covid-19, a term that has etched itself into the history of mankind still affects some people today, years later .Even in that time of despair, people found ways of solving many problems. Problems that existed before this disease, but were overlooked or even unidentified; and problems that came about after this disease.

In the midst of chaos and death, people found a way. Hard times can be good once you face it with hope. Hope that you can bring about a change that can help millions of people. The hard times you face should not be met with despair, but with HOPE! Knowing that with God all things are possible, get beside yourself and tackle every obstacle you see. The Bible says you are more than a conqueror, so act like it.

If you constantly want life to be easy, then how will you know your potential? Your potential is limited by the experiences you have and by the determination you have to endure.

**For Contemplation:**

1. Meditate on Philippians 4:13.

**NOTES:**

________________________________________

________________________________________

________________________________________

**Prayer changes things and people; make it a priority.**

# Day 346

*"Life comes to those who are a blessing to others."*

*"Give, and it shall be given unto you; good measure, pressed down, and shaken together, and running over, shall men give into your bosom. For with the same measure that ye mete withal it shall be measured to you again"* (Luke 6: 38).

There is a little song we love to sing during the offering that sums up the verse above. *"Give and it shall come back to you, good measure, press down, shaken together, running over. Give and it shall come back to you, when you give, give to the Lord."*

Yes, I know you know it, and you do the little actions with it, but do you know how profound it is? How many of us really show the blessing of God in our lives? Not only in tithes and offerings, which you should do, but do we give from what we have to others?

If you give to the poor, you lend to God. I'm sure we have heard this scripture and as children of God we must seek to do what He has commanded us. But sometimes God gives us little hints of how He blesses us, and they may not be in the form of commandments.

Today, take the opportunity to be a blessing to someone and make it your priority. It does not have to be extravagant but learn to give to others. It is better to give than to receive. As you give the Lord will continually pour into you so that your reservoir can keep on giving. Choose someone that you may not even know very well, it can be a stranger, or a children's home, or a charity. And remember to give it with love, not in the aim of getting something in return. Give out of the goodness of your heart, give as a sign to God that you are grateful for His provisions. Be a blessing to someone today, be the answer to someone's undeclared prayers.

**For Contemplation:**

1. How often do you lend to God? As you close out this year be a blessing to at least five people.

**NOTES:**

______________________________________________

______________________________________________

______________________________________________

**Prayer changes things and people; make it a priority.**

# Day 347

***" Things can leave but the power of God never leaves."***

*"And the Lord, He it is that doth go before thee; He will be with thee, He will not fail thee, neither forsake thee: fear not, neither be dismayed"* (Deuteronomy 31:8).

There is a thrill when you receive a new car, a new house or any gift. In that moment, it can feel like it is the only thing that matters. However, I have to remind you that these material possessions are not permanent. It is good to receive the blessings of the Lord, do not get me wrong, but it is bad when you idolize them over the Blesser.

The material things can never satisfy us, because after some time you will decide you want a new car again to replace the now "old" one. You will have the need to get another house, because the family has expanded. You will need to get more clothes because you have outgrown them. Things will change and things will need to be replaced, but the power of God that allowed you to receive these blessings will never leave your life. Do not get attached to material things, get attached to the power by which you received them. It is important to put the focus on Him, rather on the things you receive from Him. He has no issue with blessing you, but it is an issue if you only go to Him in expectation of receiving what He has promised. We must go to God first because we want His heart. We must go to Him with the motive of pleasing Him first. We must seek Him first, then He will add the things we need to us. We should not seek after blessings, the blessings come when we seek the Blesser. The blessings run us down, as we chase after God with all of our hearts, minds and souls.

Ensure that your life never causes the presence of God to leave. Ensure that you make every effort to let God know that you need Him more and more, each and every day. Today, just thank God for what you have; thank Him for His presence in your life. Let Him know how much you love Him. Show Him how much you love Him. Worship Him, fall down before Him. Be enveloped by the aroma of His glory. Show Yahweh, He is the Great I AM, that I AM.

**For Contemplation:**

1. What is the best physical gift you have received? Do you have the same love and adoration towards it today as the first day you received it?

**NOTES:**

---

---

---

**Prayer changes things and people; make it a priority.**

# Day 348

---

***" Persons who choose to discover the facts, will go closer to the truth."***

---

*"And ye shall know the truth, and the truth shall make you free"*( John 8:32 ).

We often live our lives based on the perceptions we have, rather than the facts. We believe that our opinions dictate the way life goes. However, if we purposefully live a life based on the truth then we will be set free.

Living life based on our perceptions causes us to have expectations, some of which can be very unrealistic. But if we choose to live life knowing that it is in the hand of God, no matter what comes, then we will not experience disappointment. The more you depend on Jesus, who is the truth, the more this truth will eventually make you free. Choose to live in the truth of God and not by your own terms.

**For Contemplation:**

1. Jesus says, "I am the way, the truth, and the life." What does this scripture mean to you? In your own words, what is the truth?

**NOTES:**

______________________________________________

______________________________________________

______________________________________________

**Prayer changes things and people; make it a priority.**

# Day 349

***" Faith operates in the intellect (mind), then your mind translates it to your body."***

*"Wherefore gird up the loins of your mind, be sober, and hope to the end for the grace that is to be brought unto you at the revelation of Jesus Christ"* (1 Peter 1:13).

Faith has the ability to change and control your mind. Once you have faith in God, then your mind will be set on a path of pleasing God. The mind then sends connections that are manifested through the body.

If you have the faith to receive something then you will put in the necessary work to achieve this. If you do not do anything, then it is not faith. Remember faith without works is dead. Therefore, whatever you desire, your faith will push you to take actions that will align you closer to what you desire. Sometimes this may take the form of doing a prophetic action, or sowing a seed, or fasting. God will instruct you on these works as the works correlate with the measure of your faith. *"Having then gifts differing according to the grace that is given to us, whether prophecy, let us prophesy according to the proportion of faith"* (Romans 12:6 ).

When you desire something, you must prophesy according to the proportion of your faith. If you have the faith for $100,000, do not prophesy to receive a million dollars. It has to be in accordance with your faith. You are the one who can limit or extend the power of God in your life. God is able to do exceeding abundantly above all that we could ask or think. Build your faith in God by learning to trust Him with everything pertaining to your life.

**For Contemplation:**

1. Begin by believing that God will take care of a bill for you. If your faith is stronger, believe Him for all your bills. The manifestation will help to build your faith.

**NOTES:**

______________________________________________

______________________________________________

______________________________________________

**Prayer changes things and people; make it a priority.**

# Day 350

---

***" Thoughts produce ways. Ways produce habits. Habits produce you."***

---

*"For as he thinketh in his heart, so is he......"* (Proverbs 23:7).

It is important to note that the Proverb says, *"As a man thinketh in his heart...".,* but why not the mind? The heart of man has a lot to do with the way he thinks. If the heart is full of love and goodness, then his thoughts will follow suit. If it is filled with hatred and evil, then only evil thoughts will arise.

You are never born the way you are today, you made yourself into who you are. Our personalities were influenced by how we were brought up, the friends we have, the morals we chose to keep and for some, the conviction of the Holy Spirit. People say they are a particular way because they were born like that. In truth, this is not so, we all chose a path based on our experiences. The response that people should have is, " I will work on it." Instead, they choose to stay in their ways.

Nevertheless, we should choose the mature way, where if we know that something offends someone we should desist from doing it. If you have the mind of Christ and the Spirit of God, then you will get your life right.

**For Contemplation:**

1. What character traits are you currently working to improve?

**NOTES:**

______________________________________________

______________________________________________

______________________________________________

**Prayer changes things and people; make it a priority.**

# Day 351

***" The strongest part of a human is the part you cannot see. It can also be the weakest."***

*"For God hath not given us the spirit of fear; but of power, and of love, and of a sound mind"*( 2 Timothy 1:7).

A mind that stays on Christ is the strongest fortress of a person. Once a person makes up their mind to do something it is very hard to deter them. This is why when a person's mind is broken, it takes the power of God to truly restore it. It is important to pray over your mind and to pray to constantly have the mind of Christ, as the pressures of life can affect you if you don't rely on Him. In Isaiah 55:8-9, our ways are not God's ways, neither are our thoughts His thoughts. But He wants us to have His ways and thoughts to live this life according to His will.

**For Contemplation:**

1. Are you sold out for God? Cast all your cares on Him and rely on Him only.

**NOTES:**

---

---

---

**Prayer changes things and people; make it a priority.**

# Day 352

---

***" When God plants His seed it will grow and flourish, even in unfavourable conditions."***

---

*"And he shall be like a tree planted by the rivers of water, that bringeth forth his fruit in his season; his leaf also shall not wither; and whatsoever he doeth shall prosper"* (Psalm 1:3).

The above scripture refers to a man who delights in the law of the Lord and meditates on it day and night. God shall make him into a tree that will bring forth fruit in its season. No matter the condition you find yourself in, once you are rooted and grounded in God, nothing by any means shall harm you or remove you from your place in Him. God does not depend on favourable conditions dictated by this earth for His power to be seen in your life. If the Lord opens the heavens above you, even in times of physical or spiritual famine, you will have plenty to eat and share.

**For Contemplation:**

1. Be still and know that He is God, and He is God all by himself. How rooted are you in God?

**NOTES:**

______________________________________________

______________________________________________

______________________________________________

**Prayer changes things and people; make it a priority.**

# Day 353

***"We can be 'spiritual' but miss GOD."***

*"Many will say to me in that day, Lord, Lord, have we not prophesied in thy name? and in thy name have cast out devils? and in thy name done many wonderful works? And then will I profess unto them, I never knew you: depart from me, ye that work iniquity"* (Matthew 7:22-23).

This is one of the most eye-opening and soul-searching scriptures in the Bible. It is one that reminds us that we cannot deceive God, He knows everything, including the intentions of our hearts. Thus we should ensure that whatever we do reflects the glory of Yahweh and He is pleased.

The things we do for God should not be as a show for others to say we are holy, as the only person who truly knows us in entirety is God. Instead, we should be working out our own salvation with fear and trembling, whilst helping others in their faith and guiding sinners to Him. We should live a life that is pleasing to Him.

If you are reading this and you have yet to give your life to Him, don't wait until the end of the year. Give your life to Him today, ask Him to enter your heart, forgive you of your sins, purify your heart and acknowledge Him as your Lord and Saviour. If you have prayed this and want to commit your life to God and be baptized, please call 876-899-2700.

For my fellow brothers and sisters in Christ, the end is fast approaching and we must be ready for His return. Keep your faith in God from wavering, even in the most difficult of times. The Lord will preserve you, keep the faith.

**For Contemplation:**

1. Minister to a soul today, whether it is a coworker or a stranger. Tell someone about the God who sees all and knows all.

**NOTES:**

________________________________________________________

________________________________________________________

________________________________________________________

**Prayer changes things and people; make it a priority.**

# Day 354

***"Your soul is the seat of your emotions, you must learn to afflict your soul."***

*"But as for me, when they were sick, my clothing was sackcloth: I humbled my soul with fasting; and my prayer returned into mine own*

*bosom"* (Psalm 35:13).

Your soul holds your emotions. If you consciously and continually humble your soul, then your emotions will be guarded by the Spirit of God. God created us with the liberty of free will, where we have the freedom of choice. Our choices eventually put us on a path of God's will, His permissive will, or our own will.

On this earth, we must learn how to afflict our souls so that we do not gratify the flesh. Your soul can either be driven by the Spirit of God if you choose or by the lust of the flesh, the eyes and the pride of life. When your body overwhelms the soul, your spirit man becomes disquieted. Your flesh /body is important, because it is the only legal entity on earth. This is why demons taught humans witchcraft and divinations because they do not have the legality to operate on earth; they need a body to possess or someone to teach. God never gave dominion over the earth to a spirit, he gave it to man, and it is through the presence and guidance of His Spirit in man that he is able to unlock his full potential of dominion in the earth.

The Holy Spirit is the greatest teacher, He will teach you all things as long as you ask and you are willing to obey Him. He will teach you how to manage your emotions.

**For Contemplation:**

1. Pray and ask the Holy Spirit to teach you each day. Journal your revelations.

**NOTES:**

______________________________________________

______________________________________________

______________________________________________

**Prayer changes things and people; make it a priority.**

# Day 355

***"You can't live your life by worrying."***

*"Therefore, I say unto you, Take no thought for your life, what ye shall eat, or what ye shall drink; nor yet for your body, what ye shall put on. Is not the life more than meat, and the body than raiment"* (Matthew 6:25)?

As you continue to trust in God, life will get easier, no matter the circumstances. In this verse, Jesus is teaching us not to worry but to know that God will provide for us and supply our needs according to His riches in glory.

Worrying signifies that you do not have your complete trust in the Father. You do not believe God is truly capable of sustaining you. God desires for us to trust Him, and to know that He will never leave us nor forsake us. All we need to do is believe. Once you are a part of God's Kingdom, the King is responsible for everything and everyone in His kingdom. Worrying will not bring anything to you.

**For Contemplation:**

1. Do you know God is a provider? Share a testimony of how God provided for you.

**NOTES:**

________________________________________________

________________________________________________

________________________________________________

**Prayer changes things and people; make it a priority.**

# Day 356

*"Effectiveness of your prayer arises when you become selfless."*

*"Confess your faults one to another, and pray one for another, that ye may be healed. The effectual fervent prayer of a righteous man availeth much"* (James 5:16).

Being selfless is a requirement that God wants us to possess. When we go to God with our requests, He is looking at the intentions of hearts. Will we help others with what He gives us? What is the purpose of having the things we ask for? As we pray for ourselves we must remember those around us as we pray to the Father. Take some time today to pray for your family, the people God has placed in your lives, leaders, community, and country.

**For Contemplation:**

1. Are your motives for asking things of God pure? How will He get the glory?

**NOTES:**

________________________________________

________________________________________

________________________________________

**Prayer changes things and people; make it a priority.**

# Day 357

*"God is always looking for return on His investments."*

*"And God blessed them, and God said unto them, Be fruitful, and multiply, and replenish the earth, and subdue it: and have dominion over the fish of the sea, and over the fowl of the air, and over every living thing that moveth upon the earth"* (Genesis 1:28).

God provides us with what we need in order to multiply. From as early as creation God has introduced the principle of investing to man. Therefore, everyone is capable of doing so. When you multiply you are walking in your purpose. As God gave Adam dominion, we must ask God what He gave us to have dominion over. Ask God for your area of specialty; what is your purpose here on earth?

**For Contemplation:**

1. Analyse your life from childhood. Write down five instances in which God provided you with what you needed to succeed.

**NOTES:**

________________________________________

________________________________________

________________________________________

**Prayer changes things and people; make it a priority.**

# Day 358

***"People will try to fight against the counsel of God in your life."***

*"There are many devices in a man's heart; nevertheless, the counsel of the Lord, that shall stand"* (Proverbs 19:21).

We must be sensitive to the voice of the Lord. He is always speaking, and we must be aware of what He is saying. The Lord will give us counsel, and it is up to us to listen, understand and obey.

To determine if you are receiving Godly counsel, ask yourself, does this align with God's words? If it doesn't then it means it cannot be from God. The Spirit of God within you will lead to where you can receive godly counsel. The counsel of God may not always be what your flesh wants to hear or accept, but I can assure you it will be beneficial to you. Seek godly counsel, and learn to listen to the voice of God.

**For Contemplation:**

1. Where no counsel is, the people fall. Always be open to Godly counsel, whether from your man of God or from the voice of God Himself. Don't ignore God's opinions on a matter.

NOTES:

______________________________________________

______________________________________________

______________________________________________

**Prayer changes things and people; make it a priority.**

# Day 359

---

*"Keep yourself in the goodness of GOD."*

---

*"Or despisest thou the riches of his goodness and forbearance and longsuffering; not knowing that the goodness of God leadeth thee to repentance"* (Romans 2:4)?

The goodness of God leads you to repentance. As you experience the goodness of God it will always remind you to be thankful to Him. Even if you err before Him, the thought about the goodness of God allows you to find yourself turning back to Him.

**For Contemplation:**

1. Plan a devotion with friends or family. Take turns sharing something that God has done for you this year.

**NOTES:**

______________________________________________

______________________________________________

______________________________________________

**Prayer changes things and people; make it a priority.**

# Day 360

***"Fear is creating false evidence of things that are not even real."***

*"I sought the Lord, and he heard me, and delivered me from all my fears"* (Psalm 34:4).

Fear is creating scenarios before they even happen. We must ask God to deliver us from our fears because fear can cripple us physically and spiritually. Once we have the Spirit of God, we should not have any fear. The scripture says perfect love casteth out all fear. Therefore, if God is within you and He is love, then fear must be expelled from your life. The fear that we must possess is the fear of the Lord, which is reverential fear. This fear causes you to live your life in a way that is pleasing unto God. The fear of the Lord will drive you away from error.

**For Contemplation:**

1. Spend 10 minutes praying and asking God to deliver you from the spirit of fear.

NOTES:

______________________________________________

______________________________________________

______________________________________________

**Prayer changes things and people; make it a priority.**

# Day 361

***"In this time where the economy of earth is shutting down, the economy of heaven will continue to be opened over life."***

*"Bring ye all the tithes into the storehouse, that there may be meat in mine house, and prove me now herewith, saith the Lord of hosts, if I will not open you the windows of heaven, and pour you out a blessing, that there shall not be room enough to receive it. And I will rebuke the devourer for your sakes, and he shall not destroy the fruits of your ground; neither shall your vine cast her fruit before the time in the field, saith the Lord of hosts. And all nations shall call you blessed: for ye shall be a delightsome land, saith the Lord of hosts"*( Malachi 3:10-12).

The church grows and prospers in difficult times. Even in times of crisis on earth, where earthly systems are affected. The church of the living God will stand. If you are a part of the Kingdom of God, you live according to the systems of heaven. The Lord will open up the windows of heaven over your life. You need to ensure that you continue to walk under the window that is opened for you. Stay within the path of God and allow His blessings to rain on you.

**For Contemplation:**

1. Practice to use the currency of faith to live and not by what you earn physically on earth.

NOTES:

______________________________________________

______________________________________________

______________________________________________

**Prayer changes things and people; make it a priority.**

# Day 362

***"You must learn to go against your nature."***

*"For I know that in me (that is, in my flesh,) dwelleth no good thing: for to will is present with me; but how to perform that which is good I find not. For the good that I would I do not: but the evil which I would not, that I do"(* Romans 7:18-19).

Learn to go against your nature. You have to be determined to stand up against the things that are not of God. We were born in sin and shapen in iniquity but it is by the grace of God and the sacrifice of Jesus Christ that we are saved and changed from this original state. We become new creatures. Do not get to the place where you are comfortable doing something that offends the Spirit of God.

When you feel like doing something that is not godly, be determined to go against the temptations that will arise. Be determined to do the good that you desire to do. Do not allow your flesh to control your actions. The actions that you do will show what is truly in control of your life. If the Spirit of God is in control then you will go against what your flesh desires.

**For Contemplation:**

1. Spend time every day praying in your heavenly language. This will help you to build your spirit man and resist the things of the flesh easier.

NOTES:

---

---

---

**Prayer changes things and people; make it a priority.**

# Day 363

***"Prophecies are ammunition that you should use to help you fight for your destiny."***

*"And they rose early in the morning, and went forth into the wilderness of Tekoa: and as they went forth, Jehoshaphat stood and said, Hear me, O Judah, and ye inhabitants of Jerusalem; Believe in the Lord your God, so shall ye be established; believe his prophets, so shall ye prosper"* (2 Chronicles 20:20).

*"We have also a more sure word of prophecy; whereunto ye do well that ye take heed, as unto a light that shineth in a dark place, until the day dawn, and the day star arise in your hearts"* (2 Peter 1:19).

The prophetic words from God that have spoken into your life must be paired with the word of God so that you can pray over your destiny. Prophetic words give guidance and a glimpse into the will of God for your life. The devil wants to prevent us from knowing who we really are and what the Lord has in store for us. He wants to steal, kill and destroy. As the words are released over your life, use them as you pray to target your life toward where God wants you to go. You must be in constant prayer for your destiny and the prophecies released over your life.

**For Contemplation:**

1. Each time you receive a prophecy pray over it, be violent for your prophecies and destiny.

NOTES:

---

---

---

**Prayer changes things and people; make it a priority.**

# Day 364

*"What is the capacity of your spiritual battery?"*

*"But ye shall receive power, after that the Holy Ghost is come upon you: and ye shall be witnesses unto me both in Jerusalem, and in all Judaea, and in Samaria, and unto the uttermost part of the earth"* (Acts 1:8 ).

Your spiritual battery should never be drained. If you feel drained, it means you have not stayed plugged into God for power. Don't wait until your battery shows warning signs. We should always remain connected to God. If we lose connection to God then our capacity to receive power from Him will have to be restored. I encourage you to take some time every day to have your personal connection with God. Yes, you may be going to church but that alone does not guarantee that you are connected to the Source of Life.

The more you stay connected the more power of the Holy Spirit will be evident in your life. As you receive power from Him, and as you offer yourself as His tabernacle to dwell in, He will shield you from the attacks of the enemy. He will keep you from every assignment that will try to disconnect you from Him. Your tomorrow depends on the power that is in you. Begin to speak the things as though they are. Speak into your tomorrow. Speak into your life with power.

**For Contemplation:**

1. Think of any mountain in your life and speak the outcome you

want, not what you think is reality.

**NOTES:**

---

---

---

**Prayer changes things and people; make it a priority.**

# Day 365

***The best way to end and begin a new year is with the Beginning and the Ending."***

*"I am Alpha and Omega, the beginning and the ending, saith the Lord, which is, and which was, and which is to come, the Almighty"* (Revelation 1:8 ).

The fact that you are reading this last page of the year, is more than enough to give God thanks. Let us just take a few moments now to reflect on the goodness of God, the challenges this year has brought, the joyous moments that have been etched in your memories forever. We give Him all the glory, and we worship Him for He is worthy.

Go ahead and just give Him thanks. We have made it, and we should never take it for granted that we are alive to see another end and another beginning. As the new year approaches, remember these points:

1. Prayer: Having a relationship with God is most important.

2. Remember to spend some time fasting to keep your soul in check.

3. Giving: practice the law of giving, and you will practice the law of kings. He that gives shall eat.

4. Practice to walk in righteousness: Be in right standing with God, and be holy, for He is holy.

5. Garner: get knowledge in your field. Go beyond what people have taught you or what they want you to learn. Whatever God is calling you to be, get more knowledge in that area.

6. Exercise discipline in all areas.

7. Practice being focused. To be focused you have to set attainable and realistic objectives, God's willing.

**For Contemplation:**

1. Look back at the things you asked God for at Day 1? What did you do to ensure the manifestation?

**NOTES:**

___

___

___

**Prayer changes things and people; make it a priority.**

# FINAL WORDS

God made humanity as a tripartite being with a body, soul, and spirit. The body is the house for our soul and spirit. With the soul, we respond to our world using our intellect, emotions and will. With our spirit we communicate with God, our Maker. If we miss this understanding, we will miss the potential power of God in our lives. As we feed our bodies with food and our mind with knowledge, we must feed our spirit with the Word of God.

The Bible says that as newborn babes, we should desire the sincere milk of the word so we may grow (1 Peter 2:2). Too many Christians are malnourished, stagnant in their spiritual growth because they belittle time spent in the Word. As weak Christians therefore, they are not able to withstand the fiery darts of the enemy. Manna-Feast has been written to provide you with spiritual food. My prayer is that you consume it with relish, making full use of the Daily Contemplations and Notes that you may be all that God intends you to be. Get the set and read them over and over, the outcome will be tremendous as you mount up on wings like eagles and become not only an overcomer, but a sharp instrument in God's hands.

Be blessed .
Rev. Dr. Otis Manning

www.ingramcontent.com/pod-product-compliance
Lightning Source LLC
Chambersburg PA
CBHW051310120626
46547CB00015B/2171
* 9 7 8 1 9 6 0 5 9 4 3 5 8 *